Better Homes and Gardens®

gifts
from the heart™

Better Homes and Gardens® Creative Collection
Des Moines, Iowa

VOLUME 2

Better Homes and Gardens®
GIFTS FROM THE HEART™
VOLUME 2

〜

editor	BECKY JOHNSTON
art director	LAUREL ALBRIGHT
editorial project coordinator	KIMBERLY O'BRIEN
copy editor	MARGARET SMITH
contributing illustrator	BARBARA GORDON
photographer	CRAIG ANDERSON
contributing project designers	LAUREL ALBRIGHT, SANDY DYE, BARBARA HICKEY, KIMBERLY O'BRIEN, MARGARET SINDELAR, JEAN WILSON
food stylist	GLENDA DAWSON
technical writer	PAM MOSTEK

〜

Better Homes and Gardens® Creative Collection™

publisher	MAUREEN RUTH
consumer product department manager	MARY HEATON
editors	EVE MAHR, NANCY WYATT
associate art director	PERRY McFARLIN
administrative assistant	MARY JOHNSON
consumer product marketing director	BEN JONES
consumer product marketing manager	KARRIE NELSON
production director	DOUGLAS M. JOHNSTON
production managers	PAM KVITNE
	MARJORIE J. SCHENKELBERG

〜

vice president, publishing director
WILLIAM R. REED

Meredith CORPORATION

chairman and CEO
WILLIAM T. KERR

〜

chairman of the executive committee
E.T. MEREDITH III

〜

Meredith Publishing Group

president	STEPHEN M. LACY
magazine group president	JERRY KAPLAN
group sales	MICHAEL BROWNSTEIN
creative services	ELLEN De LATHOUDER
manufacturing	BRUCE HESTON
consumer marketing	KARLA JEFFRIES
finance and administration	MAX RUNCIMAN

For book editorial questions, write
Better Homes and Gardens® Gifts from the Heart™ • 1716 Locust St., Des Moines, IA 50309-3023

Contents

special days

*E*ach *N*ew *S*eason of the year brings with it special days for giving gifts that express love, appreciation, or gratitude for friends and family. Throughout the year, gift-giving opportunities abound—from Valentine's Day in midwinter, Mother's Day in springtime, Father's Day in summertime, to Grandparents Day at the approach of autumn. Discover how quick, easy, and affordable it can be to treat someone special to something memorable that you've made by hand and given from the heart. Start by sharing your everlasting love on Valentine's Day by making and giving the bottles and blooms shown here and on the following pages.

bottles & blooms
page 22

bottles & blooms

Valentine's Day is the perfect opportunity to chase away the winter doldrums with a lighthearted gift of paper hearts and flowers. For love that never fades, fill apothecary bottles of all sizes and shapes with paper flowers blooming on stems of white floral wire, *page 6.* To keep cut flowers, *left* and *opposite,* fresh and upright, simply add aquarium gravel to the bottles before filling them with water. Other easy embellishments include cutting out paper hearts to use as gift tags or to personalize purchased gift bags.

**gift bag of roses
page 23**

*M*other's *D*ay is meant for making sure that Mom feels appreciated from morning to night. Start with the traditional breakfast in bed, and include a beauty bag brimming with flowers, fragrances, candles, and everything else she might dream of for a relaxing bedtime bath. Weave the bag from scraps of grosgrain and satin ribbons in assorted widths.

beauty bag

**beauty bag
page 24**

hand mirror

**hand mirror
page 25**

*F*or more Mother's Day magic, purchase a small wooden hand mirror with a stitchery insert on the back. Dress it up with woven grosgrain and satin ribbons trimmed with narrow braided cord.

heart pin

*T*ake Mother's Day to heart with a pin that says "I love you" all year-round. Simply sandwich elegant ribbon weaving between layers of Ultrasuede fabric, and add a pin back.

heart pin
page 25

lingerie keeper
page 26

sachet envelope

On Mother's Day, treat your mom to a scent sensation—a sachet envelope to tuck into a dresser drawer or to add to a bath collection. All you need is a rectangular fabric place mat with a decorative border. A few quick folds will transform it into a sachet envelope ready to fill with fragrant potpourri.

**sachet envelope
page 26**

lingerie keeper

Add a little softness to Mother's Day with a gift of luxurious silk or satin pajamas and a lace-edged lingerie bag to protect such delicate fabrics. For an almost no-sew bag, choose an elegant pillowcase with a wide decorative edge. Sew two lines of stitching on each side of the edge for a casing to hold a ribbon drawstring.

*F*ather's *D*ay calls for something new for Dad. Rather than add another tie to Dad's closet, spruce up the den with a collection of gifts that sport a North Woods theme. Focus on what he's likely to collect—remote controls for flipping channels on TV. Go all out with the chair pockets shown here, or turn the page to make it quick with an appliquéd flannel shoe bag to hold a single remote. For more organization, stack up smooth-finished log rounds on a rustic coaster chair, *page 18.*

chair pockets

**chair pockets
page 27**

coaster chair
page 28

remote holder

For a fast fix on finding the remote, iron a nature-theme motif onto a flannel shoe bag or stitch a bag from knit fabric in less time than it takes to track a moose in the woods!

**remote holder
page 28**

coaster chair

Dad will be more likely to use a coaster for his hot cup of coffee when it's within easy reach. Carry out the North Woods theme by cutting a small log into rounds. Coat the rounds with clear resin and allow to dry thoroughly; then stack them on a miniature painted wooden chair topped with a rustic crackle finish.

grandmother's brag bag

Grandparents Day will be a double delight with gifts that feature photos of the grandkids on a grandmother's brag bag and a matching wallet. Hot-glue a similar vinyl photo pocket to a man-size wallet or a checkbook cover for Granddad, and watch him beam with pride!

**brag bag
page 29**

bottles & blooms

Finished size varies.

Shown at *left* and on *page 6.*

MATERIALS

- Assorted pink, white, or peach crafting papers
- White floral or craft wires, medium weight, 12–15" in length
- Apothecary bottle
- Bath crystals
- Paper scissors
- Crafts glue

INSTRUCTIONS

1. Trace around heart patterns, *below,* onto various crafting papers. Cut out, layer, and glue together. Glue a wire to the back of each heart for a stem (see diagram, *below).*

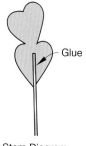

Glue

Stem Diagram

2. Fill the apothecary bottle with bath crystals (or use a purchased bottle of bath crystals).

3. Arrange the bouquet of heart flowers. Position the taller stems in the center, and trim and bend stems into a pleasing arrangement. ♥

Small Heart

Open Heart

Double Heart

Large Heart

single bloom

Finished size varies.
Shown *below* and on *page 9.*

MATERIALS

- Single bloom
- Sprig of baby's breath
- Apothecary bottle
- Aquarium gravel
- Crafting papers
- Narrow ribbon
- Crafts glue

INSTRUCTIONS

1. Fill the apothecary bottle with aquarium gravel and water. Wipe the outside of the jar dry.

2. Trim the bloom stem, leaving on the top leaves. Place in bottle, adding a little baby's breath along the side.

3. For a finishing touch, trace around heart patterns onto various crafting papers and cut out.

4. Position a 4" length of narrow ribbon around the neck of the bottle and glue the heart to the ends of the ribbon (see diagram, *below*).❤

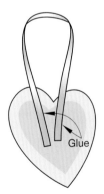

Ribbon Loop Diagram

~One More Idea~

gift bag of roses

Finished size varies.
Shown *below* and on *pages 8–9.*

MATERIALS

- 4 roses
- Sprig of baby's breath
- Apothecary bottle
- Small purchased gift bag
- Tissue paper
- Crafting paper
- Crafts glue

INSTRUCTIONS

1. From the heart patterns on *page 22,* trace and cut out one open heart and one large heart from crafting paper.

2. Glue the open heart on the large heart. Glue the layered heart to the front of the bag.

3. Fill the apothecary bottle with water; add roses and baby's breath. Dry the outside of the bottle.

4. Line the gift bag with tissue paper and place the rose bouquet in the center. Add more tissue paper around the bottle to stabilize the rose bouquet.❤

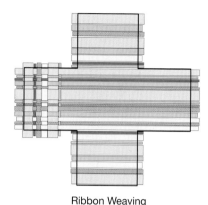

Ribbon Weaving

beauty bag

The finished bag is about 7x8". Shown *above* and on *pages 10–11*.

MATERIALS

- 28" square of fusible nonwoven firm interfacing
- 28" square of cotton print for lining
- 8 yards total of 7 to 10 colors of grosgrain and satin ribbon ranging in width from ¼" to 1½". Reserve about 3 yards of one ½" ribbon for the trim.
- Iron; press cloth
- Straight pins
- 30x30" piece of foam core board

INSTRUCTIONS

1. For horizontal weaving, cut some of the assorted ribbons into 10" and 24" pieces (they will be trimmed to measure 8" and 22"). The number of ribbons needed will vary depending on the width of the ribbon (an odd number works best).

2. Using the foam core board as a foundation, pin the lining face down, with the fusible interfacing on top and the adhesive side facing up.

3. Position the ribbons as shown in the Ribbon Base diagram, *right*. Continue placing rows of 10" ribbons until the height of the row is 7". Add the 24" pieces until they total 8" in height. Finish the horizontal layout with another section of 10" ribbons that total 7" in height. Pin to hold.

4. For weaving, cut 10" and 24" ribbon pieces. Weave short pieces through the side sections and longer pieces through the center (see Ribbon Weaving, *above right*). Alternate pulling the ribbon over and under the horizontal rows until the ribbon weaving is complete. Adjust the ribbons to fill spaces and to straighten rows. Using an iron and press cloth, fuse the woven ribbons to the fusible interfacing.

5. Unpin and remove piece from foam core board. Using the edge of the weaving as a cutting guide, trim fusible interfacing, lining, and ribbon ends (see Trim to Measurements, *below*).

6. Cut four 8½" pieces of trim ribbon to join corners. Bring up side

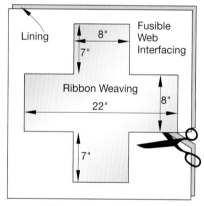

Trim to Measurements

sections and pin in place. Fold under the bottom end ½", wrap a piece of ribbon around both edges of the corner, and stitch through all layers (see diagram, *below*). Repeat to encase all corners.

7. Cut a 34" piece of trim ribbon and sew it around the top, tucking under the overlapping top end to fit.

8. For handles, cut two 10" lengths of ribbon, fold each in half, and hand-sew ends to opposite sides. ❤

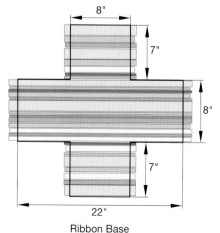

Ribbon Base

Stitch through all layers at corners.

hand mirror

Ribbon insert measures 3½" in diameter.
Shown *above* and on *page 12*.

MATERIALS

- Small wooden hand mirror with stitchery insert
- 3 yards of satin and grosgrain ribbon in assorted widths
- ½ yard of narrow cord
- Small piece of fusible interfacing
- Small piece of template plastic
- Iron; press cloth
- Hot-glue gun and hotmelt adhesive

INSTRUCTIONS

1. The length of the ribbon pieces needed for weaving will depend on the size of the mirror.

2. Cut the pieces about 4" longer than the mirror. Place the ribbons side by side on the adhesive side of the interfacing. Alternating over and under, weave ribbons until the square is complete (see diagram, *below*). Using an iron and press cloth, fuse the ribbons to the interfacing.

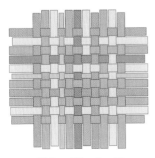

Mirror Ribbon Weaving Diagram

3. Position template plastic on the back of the mirror. Trace and cut a circle pattern about ¼" smaller than the mirror. Use the template as a cutting guide for the woven ribbon.

4. Center the template plastic on the ribbon; cut around the edge. Hot glue it to the back of the mirror. Glue cord to the edge of the ribbon.♥

Plastic template

~*One More Idea*~

heart pin

Heart pin measures 3½ " high.
Shown *above* and on *page 13*.

MATERIALS

- 2 yards total of assorted decorative ribbons in varying widths
- 12" square of Ultrasuede
- 6" square of fusible interfacing
- Pin clasp
- Iron
- Hot-glue gun and hotmelt adhesive
- Pinking shears

INSTRUCTIONS

1. Cut the assorted ribbons into 6" lengths. Place the ribbons side by side on the square of interfacing. Alternating over and under, weave the ribbons to complete the square.

2. Using an iron, fuse the ribbons to the interfacing.

3. Trace around the heart pattern *(below)* twice, for front and back, onto Ultrasuede fabric. Cut out the inside heart from the front piece and position it on the ribbon square. Machine-topstitch around the inside of the heart close to the edge.

4. Hot-glue the front to the back and trim around the outside edge with pinking shears.

5. Hand-stitch or glue a pin clasp to the back of the pin.♥

Heart Pin Pattern

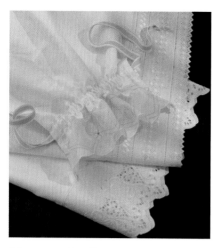

lingerie keeper

Finished size depends on pillowcase.
Shown *above* and on *page 14*.

INSTRUCTIONS

1. For each ribbon casing (one on each side of pillowcase), make two lines of machine stitching 1" apart along the decorative edging. Using a seam ripper or sharp scissors, remove the side seams between the stitching to make a casing. This will create an opening on each side to insert the ribbon.

2. Turn under the raw edges of side seams and take a few hand stitches to keep edges from fraying.

3. Cut ribbon in two pieces and insert one in each casing, using a safety pin attached to the end to push it through. Knot the two ends together on each side of bag and pull ribbons to close. ♥

sachet envelope

Finished size depends on place mat size.
Shown *above* and on *page 15*.

INSTRUCTIONS

1. Fold long sides of the place mat to meet in the center. Hand-stitch the folded edges together (see the diagrams, *below*).

2. Fold two corners together at one end to form a point. Cut a 4" (approximately) length of ribbon, fold it in half, and form a button loop. Hand-stitch the edges together, securing the ribbon loop in place at the tip of the pointed end.

3. Fold bottom toward the pointed end until the envelope is the desired size. Machine-stitch the sides through all layers.

4. Fold over the pointed end and add a decorative button that will fit through the ribbon loop. ♥

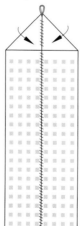
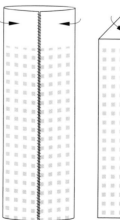
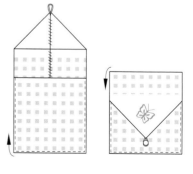

Sachet Envelope Diagrams

chair pocket

Finished size measures 42x16".
Shown *right* and on *page 17*.

MATERIALS

- ½ yard of North Woods print fabric or fabric panel for pocket
- ½ yard of North Woods print fabric for pocket lining
- 1 yard of coordinating fabric for background and background lining
- ½ yard of lightweight batting
- 2 decorative buttons
- Soft lead pencil

INSTRUCTIONS

1. Cut fabrics as shown in the Cutting Diagram, *below*.

2. To make a pocket, stitch a 9×16" piece of the North Woods print to the pocket lining, right sides facing, along the top edge.

3. Press and turn to right side. Top-stitch along the top edge.

4. Position the pocket at one end of the background fabric, matching raw edges at the bottom. Baste in place.

5. Baste batting to the wrong side of the background fabric. Stitch the background lining to the background, right sides facing, along all edges, leaving a 6" opening for turning.

6. Turn to right sides. Hand-stitch the opening edges together. Top-stitch along the edges as shown in the Assemby Diagram, *at right*.

7. With a soft lead pencil on the right side, draw two lines to divide the pocket into compartments, as shown in the Assemby Diagram, *right*. Stitch along these lines through all layers.

8. Sew a decorative button at the top of each stitching line.❤

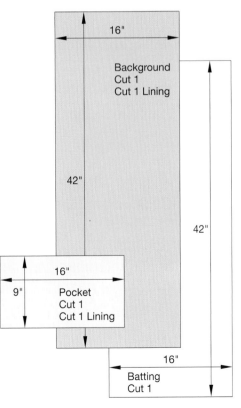

Cutting Diagram

Assembly Diagram

coaster chair

Finished size 10" high.

Shown *above* and on *page 18*.

MATERIALS

- Small wooden chair, about 10" high
- Acrylic crafts paint: cream and green
- Crackle medium
- Small log with bark, 3" in diameter
- Clear crafts resin
- Electric or band saw

INSTRUCTIONS

1. Carefully cut log into rounds that are about ½" thick.

2. Following manufacturer's instructions, coat log rounds with crafts resin. Set aside to dry.

3. Paint chair seat and back with cream paint; paint other chair parts green. Allow to dry thoroughly.

4. Apply crackle medium following manufacturer's instructions. Allow to dry.❤

remote holder

Finished size 6½x13½".
Shown on *page 19*.

MATERIALS

- 2–7x15" pieces of knit fabric or purchased flannel shoe bag
- Decorative motif cut from cotton fabric for each side of bag
- Fusible web
- 20" of cording
- Safety pin

INSTRUCTIONS

1. Enlarge the pattern from the grid, *below*.

2. With right sides together, stitch 7×15" pieces of fabric together, using a ¼" seam allowance.

3. Turn down top ¾" and stitch around edge to make casing, leaving the seam open for cording.

4. Attach a safety pin to the end of the cording and pull it through the casing. Tie ends together and turn bag right side out.

5. Following the manufacturer's instructions for fusible web, fuse motifs to each bag piece.❤

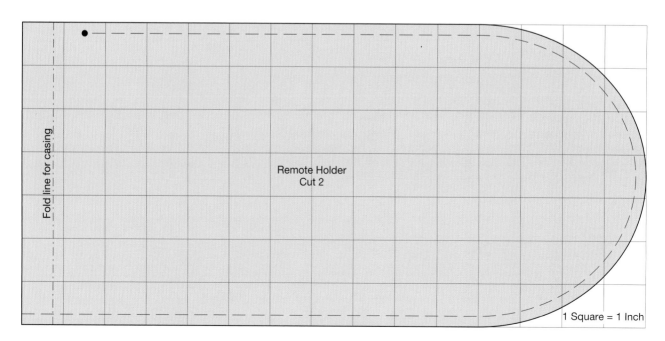

Fold line for casing

Remote Holder
Cut 2

1 Square = 1 Inch

grandmother's brag bag

The finished size will vary.

Shown *below* and on *page 21*.

MATERIALS

- Purchased canvas tote bag
- Soft transparent vinyl
- Hot-glue gun and hotmelt adhesive
- Fabric measuring tape
- Photos

INSTRUCTIONS

1. Measure the tote bag from side to side and top to bottom or the height you want. Cut a piece of vinyl to fit your measurements.

2. Position the vinyl on the bag. Secure sides and bottom with a narrow line of hot glue, leaving the top open. Slide in photos of grandchildren. ❤

wallet

Finished size varies.

Shown *right* and on *page 20*.

MATERIALS

- Purchased wallet
- Soft transparent vinyl
- Hot-glue gun and hotmelt adhesive
- Small photo

INSTRUCTIONS

1. Measure the open space of the wallet front. Cut a piece of transparent vinyl to this size.

2. Position the vinyl on the wallet. Secure sides and bottom with a narrow line of hot glue, leaving the top open. Slide in photos of grandchildren. ❤

cele

Christopher

GIFTS FOR
special
orations

Bibs for Baby are a time-honored tradition. Whether you spend hours making an heirloom lace creation or simply embellish a purchased bib, the message is "Welcome, little one!" Embroider the newborn's name on ready-made bib and burp sets or sew tiny ribbon roses to a cutwork linen bib to frame.

**framed bib art for baby
page 43**

sweet baby art

Frame Baby's first bib as a keepsake. Embellish a purchased lace-edged bib with basic embroidery and satin ribbons. Write the baby's name, weight, and birth date on crafting paper or vellum, framing the statistics in the opening of the bib.

sweet baby art
page 42

lacy baby socks

Announce the birth of twins proudly with a sampler of lacy baby socks that proclaims the arrival of your perfect pair. Embroider from the alphabet provided or one of your own on pastel linen. Layer the memento over batting before framing it.

Our
Perfect Pair

Kate

Kim

lacy baby socks
page 44

bib cards
-page 46

Birth Announcements

that celebrate Baby's arrival become frameable works of art with just a bit of fabric and ribbons. Using card stock and envelopes plus delicate trims, create tiny decorated bibs. If you like, write the child's name and the phrase "It's a girl!" or "It's a boy!"

bib cards

birthday balloons

Regardless of the number of candles on the cake, balloons say "Happy Birthday" to young and old alike. Discover how easy it is to cut semicircles for the stand-up balloons using the fold line of a blank card. Cover each balloon with a crafts-paper shape. Finish your celebration card with hand-lettering or scrapbooking alphabet letters.

birthday balloons
page 47

keepsake sports pillows

Celebrate team spirit or sports achievements with keepsake pillows made from team sweatshirts. Bring new life to an old shirt by cutting out the center motif to become a pillow front. Insert a foam pillow, and it's ready to display! Sweatshirts with hand-warmer pockets do double duty as ribbon displays for award-winning accomplishments!

**keepsake
sports pillows
page 48**

*G*raduation *D*ay is a long-awaited cause for celebration for middle school, high school, and college students. Gather up memories of the graduate's special day—from the announcement to the program—to give as a keepsake gift in a matted-to-match frame or a memory shadow box.

graduation frames

graduation frames
page 49

personalized bib

Finished size varies.

Shown *above* and on *page 30*.

MATERIALS

- Purchased baby bib
- Coordinating embroidery floss
- Soft lead pencil
- Transfer sheet

INSTRUCTIONS

1. Using the alphabet, *below*, trace the baby's name on the bib using a soft lead pencil and the transfer sheet.

2. Stitch Baby's name with embroidery floss. ♥

sweet baby art

Finished size of frame opening 10x10".

Shown *above* and on *page 32*.

MATERIALS

- White wooden or lacquered frame
- Crafting paper with pastel prints
- Sheet of vellum
- Lace bib from fabric or crafts store
- Ribbon for ties
- Embroidery floss
- Fine-tip permanent marking pen
- Hot-glue gun and hotmelt adhesive
- Brown kraft paper

INSTRUCTIONS

1. Use embroidery floss to add decorative stitching to the lace bib.

2. Cut crafting paper to fit backing board of frame. Center and glue lace bib to board.

3. Add ribbon ties to the top of the bib for the bow.

4. Write Baby's name, weight, and birth date with a permanent marking pen in the bib opening.

5. Place in the frame. Glue brown kraft paper to the back. ♥

ABCDEFGHIJKLMNOPQ

RSTUVWXYZabcdefghijklm

nopqrstuvwxyz1234567890

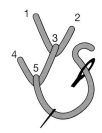

Feather Stitch

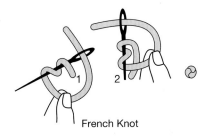

French Knot

Lazy Daisy

Straight Stitch

~One More Idea~

framed bib art

Finished size of frame opening 10x10".
Shown *above* and on *page 31*.

MATERIALS

- White wooden or lacquered frame
- Crafting paper with pastel prints
- Lace bib from fabric or crafts store
- Purchased satin appliquéd roses
- Hot-glue gun and hotmelt adhesive
- Brown kraft paper

INSTRUCTIONS

1. Cut printed crafting paper to fit backing board of frame. Center and glue lace bib to board.

2. Adhere purchased satin flowers to the bib neck opening.

3. Place in the frame. Glue brown kraft paper to the back. ♥

lacy baby socks

Finished size of frame opening 10x10".
Shown *above* and on *page 33*.

MATERIALS

- White wooden or lacquered frame
- Linen or similar fabric
- Piece of polyester batting to fit frame
- Heavy cardboard to fit frame
- Pearl cotton embroidery floss
- Embroidery hoop and needle
- White baby socks with lace and ribbon embellishments
- Heavy tape
- Hot-glue gun and hotmelt adhesive
- Brown kraft paper

INSTRUCTIONS

1. Cut linen fabric about 4" larger than the frame back. Using the lettering guide, *opposite*, trace lettering for "Our Perfect Pair" and the babies' names onto fabric. Referring to the photo for placement, embroider letters with pearl cotton floss using a stem stitch.

2. Cut a piece of cardboard and batting the same size as the frame backing. Place the batting on cardboard and center the embroidered fabric over the batting.

3. Glue the socks in place.

4. Turn the fabric edges to the back of the cardboard and tape them securely. Place the mounted socks in the frame opening. Glue brown kraft paper to the back.♥

Stem Stitch

Our
Perfect Pair

ABCDEFGHIJKL
MNOPQRSTUVW
XYZabcdefghijklmnop
qrstuvwxyz1234
567890

bib cards

Finished size of bib measures 2½" across. Shown *right* and on *page 34*.

MATERIALS

- Card stock and envelopes, available at stationery and crafts stores
- Felt or fabric scraps for bibs
- Decorative cording to match fabrics
- Purchased embroidery appliqués
- Fusible batting or interfacing
- Crafts glue
- Rotary cutter with pinking blade or scissors with decorative edge
- Optional frame or small easel

INSTRUCTIONS

1. Iron fusible batting or interfacing to the back of the fabric scraps, following manufacturer's instructions.

2. Trace bib pattern onto batting or interfacing. Cut out neck opening. Use scissors with a decorative edge or a rotary cutter with pinking blade to cut the edge of the bib (see diagram, *below)*.

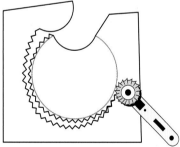

Bib Cards Cutting Diagram

3. Cut a 10" (approximately) piece of decorative cording and knot it in the center. Position ends under bib neck opening and glue in place.

4. Glue decorative appliqué onto bib.

5. Glue cording ties and bib to front of card.

6. The bib card can become art for Baby by placing it in a frame or on a small easel. ❤

Bib Cards Pattern

birthday balloons

Finished size 7x9".

Shown *left* and on *page 36*.

MATERIALS

- 7x9" piece of heavy card stock
- 5—2" squares of soft patterns in vellum scrapbooking paper
- Silver gel pen
- Fine-tipped black marking pen
- Crafts scissors
- Crafts knife
- Soft lead pencil

INSTRUCTIONS

1. Draw a light pencil line at the lengthwise center of the card.

2. Using the balloons shown, *below*, as guides, cut out balloons from vellum scrapbooking paper. Glue in place.

3. Using the crafts knife, cut out the tops of balloons as shown. Score the card between the balloons and fold.

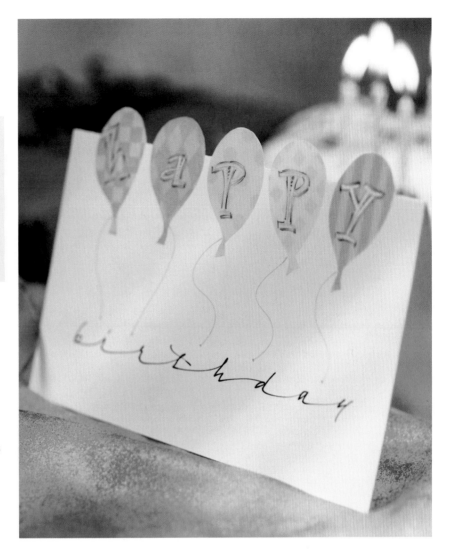

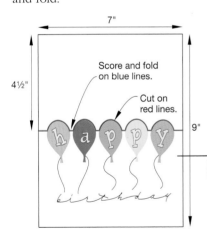

4. Spell out "happy" on the balloons and draw strings using the silver gel pens.

5. With the black marker, write "birthday" at the bottom. ❤

keepsake sports pillows

Finished size 16x16".

Shown *above* and on *page 38*.

MATERIALS

- Team sweatshirts or T-shirts
- 16" pillow form
- Sewing machine
- Sport awards and memorabilia

INSTRUCTIONS

1. Center the team name or logo within a 17" square. If you use a sweatshirt with pockets, center the pockets near the lower edge of the 17" square. Cut out the 17" square using the front and back of the sweatshirt or T-shirt. If desired, add medals, letters, or pins to the pillow front.

2. Layer shirt squares right sides together. Using a ½" seam allowance, machine-stitch around three edges, leaving one side open to insert the pillow form.

3. Fold under ½" along the opening. Press. Insert pillow and hand-stitch to close the opening. ❤

Cutting Diagram

graduation frames

Finished sizes vary.
Shown *above* and *right,* and on
pages 40–41.

MATERIALS

- Decorator wood picture frame
  with nonglare glass
- Coordinating photo mat
- Coordinating mat board
- Graduation memorabilia such as
  programs, photos, tassels,
  pins, special awards
- Crafts glue

INSTRUCTIONS

1. Arrange graduation memorabilia
collage-style on the mat board.

2. Glue lightly in position.

3. Layer photo mat over collage.

4. Place in frame and secure the
frame back. ❤

harvest candle ring
page 60

GIFTS FROM
nature

The Seasons come full circle, and a harvest candle ring gift announces the arrival of autumn. To make the candle, fill a glass canning jar with tiny gourds, ornamental corn, and strawflowers. Add candle oil and a candlewick. Center the jar in a twig wreath that overflows with more of nature's bounty.

autumn wreath

Gather fall foliage by the armloads or buy it by the bagful for a wreath that will be a welcome addition to autumn decor anywhere. Here, a garland of purchased autumn leaves in deep hues of rust and green graces a heart-shape grapevine wreath.

**autumn wreath
page 61**

autumn glow

For an informal centerpiece that's light and airy, give a gift that glows with the colors of autumn. Maple leaves cascade across a candle-filled hurricane lamp as a tribute to autumn's glory.

autumn glow
page 61

oak leaves
& acorns projects
page 62

*N*ature comes to the table in the shapes of oak leaves and acorns. This impressive collection of autumn accessories includes oak leaf place mats and napkins, copper-coil-and-leaf napkin rings, acorn coasters, and a patchwork runner. These fabric accents are sure to delight someone on your gift list.

oak leaves
& acorns

nature's bounty

umpkins, plain or fancy, are an irresistible

splash of seasonal color and a natural

for autumn gift-giving. The smiling ceramic

jack-o'-lanterns, *opposite,* and the flower-

filled Fun-Kins, *below,* look freshly

harvested but will

last much longer than

pumpkins picked

from the patch.

**jack-o'-lanterns
page 67**

party favors

Leaf-embellished peat pot pails and terra-cotta pots painted to look like jack-o'-lanterns are brimming with treats for your party guests. These festive favors hold cellophane bags of Savory Nuts, Trail Mix with Candy Corn, and Caramel Corn Party Mix. For a quick and easy farewell treat, give guests a jar of Pesto Popcorn Seasoning to take home.

jack-o'-lantern pots
page 69

harvest candle ring

Finished size varies.

Shown *left* and on *page 50*.

MATERIALS

- Lamp oil
- 6" of fiberglass candlewick
- Gourds, dried ornamental corn, pinecones, and strawflowers for wreath and jar
- Spanish moss
- Raffia for bow
- Round twig wreath from crafts stores
- Hammer and heavy nail
- Hot-glue gun and hotmelt adhesive or floral glue

INSTRUCTIONS

1. Arrange gourds, corn, and strawflowers in the jar. Pour in lamp oil to within 1" from the jar top. It may be necessary to adjust the contents of the jar slightly as you pour the oil.

2. Using the hammer and nail, punch a hole in the jar lid. Place the lid on the jar and add the jar ring. Insert the candlewick. Tie a raffia bow around the neck of the jar.

3. Place a layer of Spanish moss on the top of the wreath and secure it with glue. Arrange and glue corn, gourds, pinecones, and dried flowers onto the moss to cover and spill over the edges of the wreath. ♥

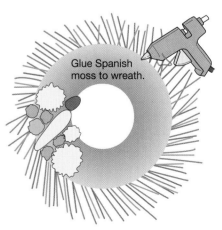

Glue Spanish moss to wreath.

autumn leaves wreath

Finished size varies.

Shown *above* and on *page 52*.

MATERIALS

- Heart-shape grapevine wreath from a crafts store
- Garland of autumn leaves
- Hot-glue gun and hotmelt adhesive or floral glue
- Crafts scissors

INSTRUCTIONS

1. Carefully cut the assorted leaves from the garland.

2. Place several drops of glue on the center of the leaves and position them on the grapevine wreath. Overlap and tuck the leaves for a pleasing arrangement. ♥

autumn glow

Finished size varies.

Shown *above* and on *page 53*.

MATERIALS

- Clear glass hurricane lamp
- Clear glass plate
- Purchased decorative paper autumn leaves from crafts stores
- Decoupage medium
- Paintbrush
- Candle

INSTRUCTIONS

1. Following the decoupage manufacturer's instructions, decoupage paper leaves in a circle on the plate. Add a small amount of decoupage glue under the leaves to secure them on the curved surface.

2. Randomly decoupage paper leaves to the hurricane lamp.

3. When the lamp and plate are thoroughly dry, place a candle in the center of the lamp. ♥

Overlap leaves

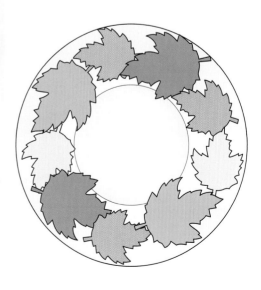

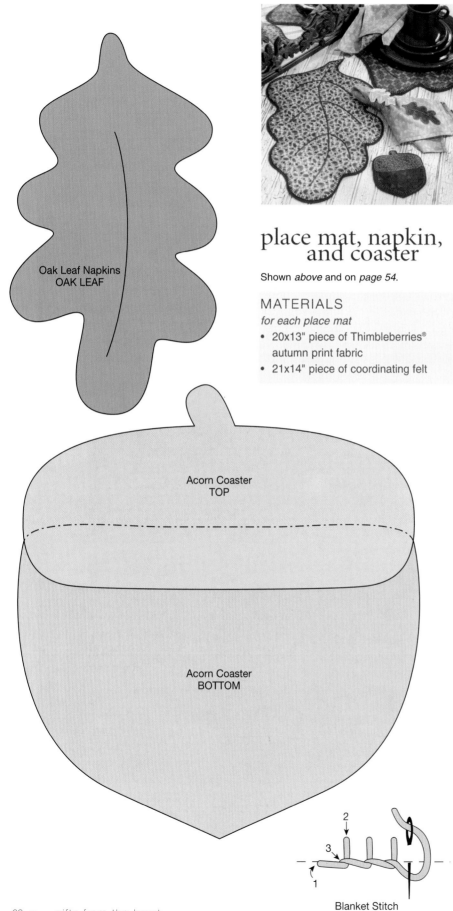

Oak Leaf Napkins
OAK LEAF

Acorn Coaster
TOP

Acorn Coaster
BOTTOM

place mat, napkin, and coaster

Shown *above* and on *page 54.*

MATERIALS

for each place mat
- 20x13" piece of Thimbleberries® autumn print fabric
- 21x14" piece of coordinating felt

- Coordinating pearl cotton for blanket stitching
- 21x13" piece of fusible web
for each napkin
- 16" square of print cotton to coordinate with place mat
- 16" square of print fabric for lining
- Fabric for leaf appliqué
- Fusible web
- Coordinating pearl cotton for blanket stitching
- Contrasting thread
for each coaster
- 6" square of felt
- Coordinating cotton fabric
- Fusible web
- Coordinating pearl cotton

INSTRUCTIONS

1. *For each place mat,* trace large oak leaf pattern onto fusible web. Fuse fabric and cut out. Place on felt piece and blanket-stitch by hand or machine around the edges. Use a sewing machine and contrasting thread to stitch along the center and side veins of the leaf. Trim felt around the leaf edge, leaving a generous ¼" edging.

2. *For each napkin,* trace leaf pattern onto fusible web. Following the manufacturer's directions, fuse webbing to cotton fabric. Cut out leaf and fuse it to a napkin corner. Referring to the pattern for placement, embroider the vein with pearl cotton using a stem stitch. Blanket-stitch by hand or machine around the edges, referring to diagram, *below.* With right sides together, sew napkin top to lining around all edges, leaving a 6" opening on one side for turning. Turn right side out. Press. Hand-stitch opening closed.

3. *For each coaster,* trace each section of acorn pattern onto fusible web. Fuse to fabric and cut out. Overlap section edges and position onto felt. Fuse in place. Blanket-stitch around edges and trim the edge. ❤

Blanket Stitch

Stem Stitch

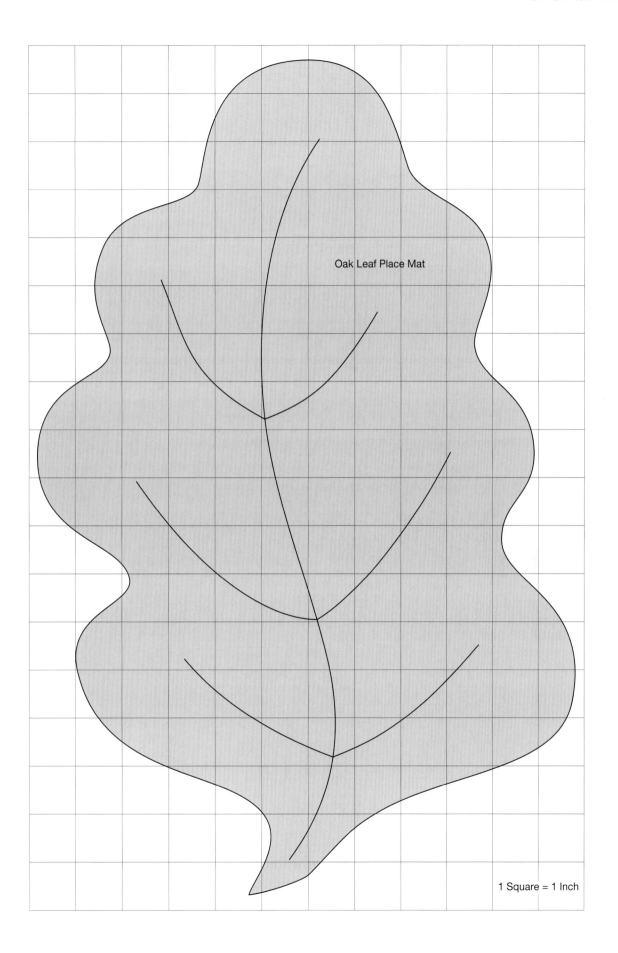

Oak Leaf Place Mat

1 Square = 1 Inch

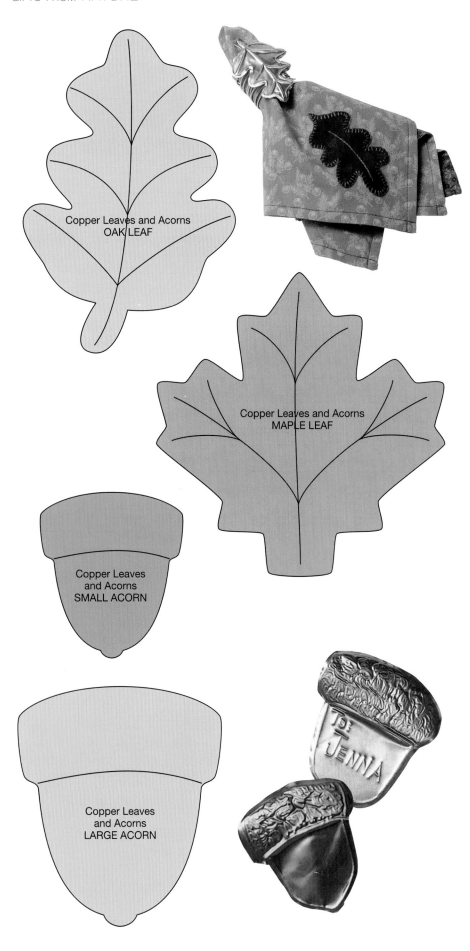

Copper Leaves and Acorns
OAK LEAF

Copper Leaves and Acorns
MAPLE LEAF

Copper Leaves
and Acorns
SMALL ACORN

Copper Leaves
and Acorns
LARGE ACORN

napkin ring

Finished size varies.
Shown *left* and on *page 54*.

MATERIALS

- Copper foil sheets
- Copper wire
- Soft lead pencil
- Template plastic
- Crafts scissors
- Crafts paintbrush
- Paper towel tube

INSTRUCTIONS

1. Trace around leaf patterns onto template plastic and cut out.

2. Trace leaves onto copper foil with a soft lead pencil and cut out the shapes. Add veins with the handle end of the paintbrush, applying light pressure.

3. Preheat oven to 250°F. Bake leaf about 10 minutes. For darker color, leave in longer.

4. Loosely wrap copper wire around cardboard tube about 7 times, forming a coil.

5. Position leaf on the coiled wire. Bend stem under wire to secure. Pull the napkin through the coil.❤

gift tag

Finished size varies. Shown *left*.

MATERIALS

- Copper foil
- Soft lead pencil
- Template plastic
- Crafts paintbrush

INSTRUCTIONS

1. Trace around acorn pattern onto template plastic and cut out.

2. Place acorn template onto copper foil, trace, and cut out.

3. Bake as in Step 3 above.

4. Using a paintbrush handle, add details, outlines, and names.❤

autumn patchwork runner

Finished size 24½x16½".

Shown *right* and on *page 55*.

MATERIALS

- ¾ yard tan medium print fabric
- 1 yard tan small print fabric
- ¼ yard dark brown fabric
- 20x7" lightweight cotton batting
- Coordinating thread
- Rotary cutter and cutting mat
- Acrylic ruler

Cut the following pieces from the tan medium print fabric

- 1—2x42" strip for checkerboard corners
- 3—2x42" strips for binding
- 1—10½x18" center piece

Cut the following pieces from the tan small print fabric

- 2—3½x15½" border pieces
- 2—3½x7½" border pieces
- 1—20x27" piece for the backing

Cut the following pieces from the dark brown fabric

- 1—2x42" strip for checkerboard corners

INSTRUCTIONS

1. With right sides together, sew one tan 2×42" strip to one dark brown 2×42" strip along the long edge using a ¼" seam allowance. Press the seam toward the dark brown fabric. Using the acrylic ruler and rotary cutter, cut the strip set into sixteen 2" segments (see Diagram 1).

Diagram 1

2. Join two segments, reversing colors, as shown in Diagram 2, *below*. Repeat to make eight four-patch units (see Diagram 3).

Diagram 2   Diagram 3

3. Positioning segments as shown in Diagram 4, sew segments to the ends of the border strips.

Diagram 4

4. Sew a four-patch unit to each end of the long border strips. Assemble the runner as shown in Diagram 5.

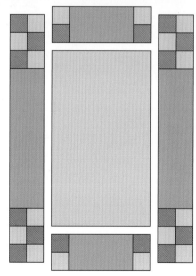

Diagram 5

5. Layer the runner top, batting, and backing. Pin or baste and machine-quilt as desired.

6. Sew binding to finish the runner.❤

flower mug coaster

Finished size 4½x5½".

Shown *left* and on *page 55*.

MATERIALS

- 7" square of cotton print fabric
- 8" square of coordinating felt
- Scrap of fabric for flower center
- 8" square of fusible web
- Pearl cotton embroidery floss to coordinate with flower and center
- Embroidery needle with a large eye

INSTRUCTIONS

1. Trace flower pattern onto fusible web. Fuse to cotton fabric and cut out.

2. Position onto felt square and fuse with an iron.

3. Using the edge of the flower as a guide, trim felt to about ¼" beyond fabric.

4. Blanket-stitch with pearl cotton embroidery floss around the edge of the flower. ♥

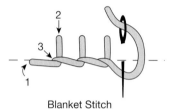

Blanket Stitch

Flower Coaster Pattern

jack-o'-lanterns

Finished sizes vary.
Shown *above* and on *page 56*.

MATERIALS

- Fresh or terra-cotta pumpkins, or Fun-Kins artificial pumpkins
- Dried florals in autumn colors
- Acrylic craft paint in orange and green
- Fabric scrap for hatband
- Candles

INSTRUCTIONS

1. *For the pumpkin candleholder,* paint terra-cotta pumpkin orange and hat green. Tie a fabric scrap around the top as a hatband. Place candle inside.

2. *For the ceramic or terra-cotta pumpkin bouquet,* invert the lid and place the floral arrangement so that it rests snugly in the lid. Place candle inside the pumpkin. ❤

~One More Idea~

flower-filled pumpkin

Finished sizes vary.
Shown *right* and on *page 56*.

MATERIALS

- Fresh pumpkin, or Fun-Kins artificial pumpkin
- Fresh florals in autumn colors

INSTRUCTIONS

1. For pumpkin bouquet, cut off the top of the pumpkin.

2. Place the floral arrangement in the pumpkin so that it rests snugly in the opening. ❤

peat pot pails

Finished sizes vary.
Shown *left* and on *page 58*.

MATERIALS

- Peat pots in various sizes from a garden shop
- 18-gauge copper wire
- Leaf cutouts from a crafts store
- Decoupage medium
- Nail for punching hole in pots
- Cellophane bags
- Decorative ribbon
- One recipe Savory Nuts *(left)*
- One recipe Pesto Popcorn Seasoning *(left)*
- One recipe Caramel Corn Party Mix *(below)*

INSTRUCTIONS

1. Following manufacturer's instructions, decoupage leaves to the sides of peat pots and allow to dry. Using a nail, punch two holes opposite each other in the pots and insert a strip of copper wire for a handle. Twist the ends of the wire to secure.

2. Fill cellophane bags with treats, tie with a decorative ribbon, and place in the pots. ♥

savory nuts

Shown *above* and on *page 58*.

INGREDIENTS

- 2 tablespoons white wine Worcestershire sauce
- 1 tablespoon olive oil
- 2 tablespoons snipped fresh thyme or ½ teaspoon dried thyme, crushed
- 1 teaspoon snipped fresh rosemary or ¼ teaspoon dried rosemary, crushed
- ¼ teaspoon salt
- ⅛ teaspoon ground red pepper
- 2 cups macadamia nuts, broken walnuts, and/or unblanched almonds

INSTRUCTIONS

1. Combine Worcestershire sauce, olive oil, thyme, rosemary, salt, and ground red pepper.

2. Spread nuts in a 13×9×2-inch baking pan. Drizzle with oil mixture. Toss gently.

3. Bake in a 350°F oven for 12 to 15 minutes or until nuts are toasted, stirring occasionally. Spread on a large sheet of foil; cool.

4. Store in an airtight container. Makes 2 cups. ♥

pesto popcorn seasoning

Shown *above* and on *page 58*.

INGREDIENTS

- 3 tablespoons butter-flavored sprinkles
- 2 tablespoons grated Parmesan cheese
- 1 teaspoon dried basil, crushed
- ½ teaspoon dried parsley flakes, crushed
- ⅛ to ¼ teaspoon garlic powder

INSTRUCTIONS

1. Combine all ingredients in a small bowl. Store mix in the refrigerator. Seasoning mixture will coat about 10 cups of popped popcorn.

2. For gift giving, pour the seasoning mix into a 4-ounce-size bottle. *Note:* Include instructions to keep refrigerated. ♥

caramel corn party mix

Shown *above* and on *page 58*.

INGREDIENTS

- 4 cups popped popcorn
- 2 cups bite-size wheat or bran square cereal
- 1½ cups small pretzels or pretzel sticks
- 1½ cups pecan halves
- ¾ cup packed brown sugar
- 6 tablespoons butter (no substitutes)
- 3 tablespoons light-color corn syrup
- 1 teaspoon pumpkin pie spice
- ¼ teaspoon baking soda
- ¼ teaspoon vanilla
- Dash ground red pepper

INSTRUCTIONS

1. Heat oven to 300°F. Remove all unpopped kernels from popped popcorn. Combine popcorn, cereal, pretzels, and pecans in a 17×12×2-inch baking or roasting pan.

2. Mix brown sugar, butter, and corn syrup in a medium saucepan. Cook and stir with a wooden spoon over medium heat until mixture boils. Reduce heat to medium-low. Cook without stirring for 5 minutes more.

3. Remove pan from heat. Stir in pumpkin pie spice, baking soda, vanilla, and ground red pepper. Pour over popcorn mixture in pan, gently stirring to coat. Bake for 15 minutes. Stir mixture; bake 5 minutes more. Spread caramel corn mixture on a large piece of buttered foil to cool. Break into pieces. Store tightly covered for up to 1 week. Makes about 8 cups.

jack-o'-lantern pots

Finished sizes vary.

Shown *right* and on *page 59*.

MATERIALS

- Small terra-cotta pots
- Acrylic crafts paint: orange and black
- Medium-weight wire for handles
- Electric drill and masonry drill bit
- Cellophane bags
- Raffia
- Granola treats

INSTRUCTIONS

1. Paint pots with orange paint and let dry thoroughly. Draw on pumpkin faces and paint the faces black.

2. Drill a small hole in each side of a pot using an electric drill and masonry bit. Cut wire the desired length for handles and insert one end of wire through each hole from the inside. Bring up to top of pot and twist to secure.

3. Fill cellophane bags with granola, tie the tops with raffia, and place in the pumpkin pots. ❤

Jack-o'-Lantern Pots

trail mix with candy corn

Shown *above* and on *page 59*.

INGREDIENTS

- 4 cups granola
- 1 6-ounce package mixed dried fruit bits or 1⅓ cups raisins
- 1 cup peanuts, broken walnuts, or pecans
- 1½ cups mixture of any of the following: shelled sunflower seeds, coconut, candy-coated milk chocolate pieces, candy-coated peanut butter-flavored pieces, candy-coated fruit-flavored pieces, or candy corn

INSTRUCTIONS

1. In a large bowl, combine all ingredients; toss to mix.

2. Store in an airtight container in a cool, dry place. Makes 8 cups. ❤

bottles in a basket
page 80

GIFTS FROM THE
kitchen

*B*ottles in a *B*asket—what could be more appetizing than food gifts from your kitchen? For your next hostess gift, fill pretty bottles with fruit-flavored or chive-onion vinegars. Wrap the bottles in cloth napkins and set them in a basket trimmed with generous-size tassels.

**table runner
page 81**

ice cream sauces

Sweeten any gathering with a gift of sauces for dessert.

Homemade Hot Fudge Sauce and Caramel-Rum Sauce are

delicious ice cream toppers or tasty dips for fresh berries.

**ice cream sauces
page 82**

appetizers to go

Get compliments by the cartful with these appetizers to go.

Red and green country carts carry gift jars of Lemony Marinated

Antipasto and Fiery Marinated Olives.

appetizers to go
page 82

farmer's market
stockpot
page 84

farmer's market stockpot

Newlyweds or someone setting up housekeeping for the first time will welcome this gift. Start with a stockpot large enough to hold everything needed for soup—from stirring to serving! Fill it with an inexpensive place setting for four, fringed napkins, and a jar of lentil soup starter mix. Include the recipes for soup and tasty olive breadsticks. Toss in an opera-length oven mitt for safe stirring and some wooden spoons that are sure to bring satisfied soup-sipping smiles.

ack a picnic gift basket presto with this winning combination of easily embellished accessories and homemade picnic fare. Perk up a plain basket with a border of miniature ladybugs and decorate wooden napkin rings with paint and butterflies from the crafts store. Make a jar of Refrigerator Squash Pickles and a plate of Chocolate Revel Bars, including recipes, as a bonus treat.

picnic in a basket

picnic in a basket
page 86

Friends come into our
lives and quickly go.
Some stay for a while
leaving footprints on our hearts
and we are forever
changed.

box of hearts
page 88

box of hearts

*H*eart-shape boxes and cookies are sure to bring heartfelt thanks from everyone on your gift list. Cutout cookies, *opposite,* are bright and shiny with paintbrush icing. For more fun, paint matching small wooden gift tag hearts, *below,* and write messages of friendship on the box lids.

3. Line a colander with several layers of 100% cotton cheesecloth. Strain vinegar mixture through the colander and let it drain into a bowl. Discard fruit. Transfer strained vinegar to a clean 1-pint glass jar or bottle. If desired, add a few additional pieces of fresh fruit to the jar or bottle. Cover jar or bottle tightly with a nonmetallic lid (or cover with plastic wrap and then seal tightly with a metal lid). Store vinegar in a cool, dark place for up to 6 months. Makes about 1½ cups (24 tablespoon-size servings).

Note: For gift giving, include instructions to keep refrigerated.❤

chive-onion vinegar

Shown *left* and on *page 70.*

INGREDIENTS
- 2 cups white wine vinegar or rice vinegar
- 1 tablespoon snipped fresh chives
- 1 green onion, chopped
- 2—3- to 4-inch strips of lemon peel
- 1 whole green onion

INSTRUCTIONS
1. In a clean 1-quart glass jar, combine vinegar, chives, chopped onion, and lemon peel. Cover with plastic wrap; refrigerate for 1 week, stirring once a day. Pour vinegar-chive mixture through a fine-mesh strainer; drain into a bowl. Discard solids.
2. Transfer strained vinegar to a clean 1-quart jar or bottle. Add whole green onion to jar. Cover tightly with a nonmetallic lid (or cover with plastic wrap and tightly seal with a metal lid). Store in refrigerator for up to 6 months. Makes about 2 cups.

Note: For gift giving, include instructions to keep refrigerated.❤

bottles in a basket

Finished size varies.
Shown *above* and on *page 70.*

MATERIALS
- Purchased basket
- Tall bottles with stoppers
- Cloth napkins
- Decorative tassels

INSTRUCTIONS
1. Fill the bottles with vinegars from the recipes that follow, *right.*
2. Wrap bottles with cloth napkins and place in the basket.
3. Tie or loop decorative tassels around the basket handle.❤

fruit-flavored vinegars

(choose strawberry or blueberry)

Shown *above* and on *page 70.*

INGREDIENTS
- 1 cup fresh strawberries or 1 cup fresh blueberries
- 2 cups white wine vinegar

INSTRUCTIONS
1. In a small stainless-steel or enamel saucepan, combine fruit and vinegar. Bring to a boil; reduce heat. Boil gently, uncovered, for 3 minutes. Remove from heat and cover loosely with cheesecloth; cool.
2. Pour mixture into a clean 1-quart jar. Cover jar tightly with a nonmetallic lid (or cover with plastic wrap and then seal tightly with a metal lid). Let stand in a cool, dark place for 2 weeks.

table runner

Finished sizes 16×30".
Shown on *page 71*.

MATERIALS

- 1 yard of brown print fabric
- 2½ yards of cording in a coordinating color
- Two purchased tassels
- Decorative brass button
- Sewing scissors

INSTRUCTIONS

1. Cut two pieces of fabric as shown in Cutting Diagram, *below*.

2. Pin the cording to the top, aligning the cording as shown in Diagram 1. Baste.

3. With right sides together, place backing on top and pin (see Diagram 2). Using a ¼" seam, stitch around all sides, leaving a 6" opening for turning.

4. Turn, press, and hand-stitch the opening closed.

5. Sew a button and tassels to the pointed end of the table runner. ♥

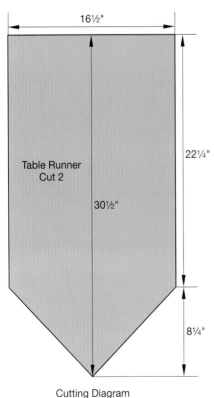

16½"

22¼"

Table Runner
Cut 2

30½"

8¼"

Cutting Diagram

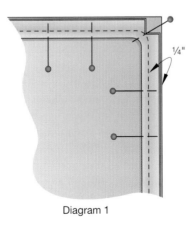

¼"

Diagram 1

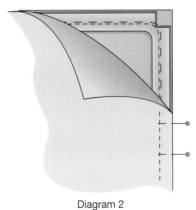

Diagram 2

fiery marinated olives

Shown *above* and on *page 73*

hot fudge sauce

Shown *above* and on *page 72*

INGREDIENTS

- 8 ounces semisweet chocolate pieces (1⅓ cups)
- ½ cup butter
- 1⅓ cups sugar
- 1⅓ cups whipping cream

INSTRUCTIONS

1. Melt chocolate and butter in a heavy medium saucepan over low heat, stirring frequently. Add sugar. Gradually add whipping cream. Bring to boiling; reduce heat. Boil gently over low heat for 8 minutes, stirring frequently. Remove from heat. Let stand at room temperature until cool.

2. For gift giving, pour into half-pint jars. Seal and label. Store sauce in the refrigerator for up to 2 months.

3. On the gift tag or label, include directions to reheat the fudge sauce in a small saucepan over medium-low heat and serve over ice cream. Makes 4 half-pints (about 3½ cups).

Note: Include instructions to keep refrigerated.❤

caramel-rum sauce

Shown *above* and on *page 72*

INGREDIENTS

- 2 cups packed brown sugar
- ¼ cup cornstarch
- 1⅓ cups half-and-half or light cream
- 1 cup water
- ½ cup light-color corn syrup
- ¼ cup butter
- ¼ cup rum
- 2 teaspoons vanilla

INSTRUCTIONS

1. Combine brown sugar and cornstarch in a heavy large saucepan. Stir in half-and-half or light cream, water, and corn syrup. Cook and stir over medium heat until thickened and bubbly (mixture may look curdled). Cook and stir 2 minutes more. Remove from heat. Stir in butter, rum, and vanilla. Let mixture stand at room temperature until cool.

2. For gift giving, pour into half-pint jars. Seal and label. Store sauce in the refrigerator for up to 2 months. Makes 4 half-pints (about 3½ cups).

Note: Include instructions to keep refrigerated.❤

INGREDIENTS

- 2—3-ounce jars almond-stuffed olives, drained
- ⅓ cup salad oil
- ¼ cup water
- 3 tablespoons lime juice
- 1 tablespoon snipped cilantro
- 1 tablespoon crushed red pepper
- 1 teaspoon cumin seed
- 1 clove garlic, minced

INSTRUCTIONS

1. In a small saucepan, combine all ingredients. Bring to a boil; reduce heat. Simmer, covered, 5 minutes. Remove from heat. Cool.

2. Use a slotted spoon to transfer olives to jars with tight-fitting lids. Pour cooked liquid over olives. Cover and chill in refrigerator for 4–7 days before serving. Store in refrigerator for up to 3 weeks. Makes about 2 cups.

Note: Include instructions to keep refrigerated.❤

lemony marinated antipasto

Shown *above* and on *page 73*

INGREDIENTS

- 1 pound spicy Italian chicken or turkey sausage links
- 1 tablespoon cooking oil

- ⅓ cup olive oil
- 2 teaspoons finely shredded lemon peel
- ⅓ cup lemon juice
- 2 tablespoons snipped fresh basil leaves
- 2 teaspoons dried Italian seasoning, crushed
- 2 cloves garlic, minced
- 1—12-ounce jar roasted red sweet peppers, drained
- 12 ounces mozzarella cheese, cut into ½-inch cubes
- 1 cup pitted kalamata olives

INSTRUCTIONS

1. Cook sausage links in cooking oil in a medium skillet over medium heat for 10 minutes or until cooked through, turning frequently to brown evenly. Remove sausage from heat and allow to cool. Cut into ¼-inch slices and set aside.

2. For dressing, whisk together olive oil, lemon peel, lemon juice, snipped basil, Italian seasoning, and garlic in a small bowl; set aside. Cut roasted red peppers into bite-size strips.

3. Layer sausage, red pepper strips, cheese, and olives in a 2-quart jar or two 1-quart jars. Pour dressing into jar(s), cover tightly, and refrigerate for 1 to 2 days. Turn jar(s) upside down occasionally to distribute the dressing.

4. Let stand at room temperature for 30 minutes before serving. Makes 12 to 16 servings.

Note: Include instructions to keep refrigerated.❤

red & green carts

Finished size of red cart is 5½×11" and green cart is 7×11½"
Shown *opposite* and on *page 73*.

MATERIALS
for red cart
- 10x10" piece of ⅜" plywood
- 2½" piece of ⅛"-diameter dowel
- Four 1¾"-diameter pine wheels
- Four ¾x2⅜" axle pins
- 2¾" piece of 16-gauge wire

for green cart
- 12" length of 1x12 clear pine
- Four 2"-diameter pine wheels
- Four ⅜x3" axle pins
- One ¼x36" leather strip
for both carts
- Scroll saw or band saw
- Sandpaper; transfer paper
- Drill with bits
- Red and green acrylic paints
- Eight ⅜" washers

INSTRUCTIONS
red cart

1. Enlarge tongue pattern, *lower right*. Transfer to plywood. On remainder of plywood, mark a 5¼×8¾" base, a ¾×5½" rear wheel, back brace, and a ¾" handle; cut out. Sand all pieces until smooth.

2. On the outer edges of tongue and back brace, mark and drill a ¹⁵⁄₆₄"-diameter hole 2" deep. Using a ⁷⁄₆₄" bit, drill through the front of tongue as indicated by dotted lines on diagram and through handle ¼" from each short end.

3. To assemble body, wood-glue the tongue to the bottom of the base, aligning dotted end with one short edge of base. Glue the back brace to the other base end, with the edge of the brace closest to the back ⅝" from and parallel to the edge.

4. Slide the dowel through the hole in one end of the handle until centered; glue. Insert wire through one hole in the tongue end, the remaining handle hole, then the other tongue hole. Center wire and bend ends to underside of the tongue.

5. Paint body, handle dowel, axle pins, and wheel centers red. Paint remainder of wheels green. Lightly sand all pieces to create an aged effect. Seal with polyurethane. Allow to dry.

6. Insert axles through wheel centers, then through the washers. Use wood glue to glue axles into the holes in the sides of the base.

green cart

1. Enlarge base pattern, *below.* Transfer to pine; cut out. Sand all pieces until smooth.

2. Measure and mark each side of the base 2" and 7" from the back edge of the cart. Drill a hole 2" deep at each mark. Also mark top of base ¾" from center front. Drill all the way through base.

3. Paint the base, axle pins, and wheel centers green. Paint the remainder of wheels red. Lightly sand all pieces to create an aged effect; seal with polyurethane. Allow to dry.

4. Insert axles through wheels, then through the washers. Use wood glue to glue axles into holes in sides of base.

5. Insert the leather strip into the opening at the base front. Tie leather in a knot at the base bottom.❤

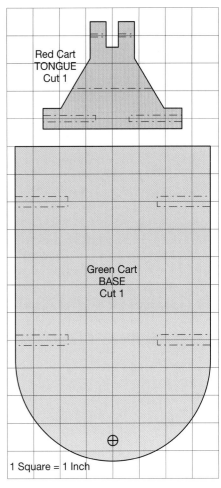

Red Cart
TONGUE
Cut 1

Green Cart
BASE
Cut 1

1 Square = 1 Inch

opera-length oven mitt

Finished size 18x8".
Shown *above* and on *page 74*.

MATERIALS
- ½ yard quilted cotton fabric for oven mitt
- Bias tape to match quilted fabric

INSTRUCTIONS
1. To make oven mitt, fold fabric right sides together and trace around oven mitt pattern onto top layer. Cut out through both layers.
2. Right sides together, stitch around edges with a ⅜" seam, leaving an opening. Following manufacturer's instructions, sew bias tape around the wrist opening. ❤

fringed napkins

Finished size 18x18".
Shown *above* and on *page 74*.

MATERIALS
- 18" square woven plaid fabric for each napkin

INSTRUCTIONS
1. Tightly stitch ½" from all edges of 18" woven fabric.
2. Pull and remove threads between stitching and fabric edge to make fringe. ❤

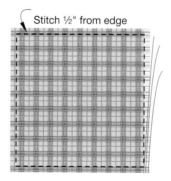

Stitch ½" from edge

lentil stew

Shown *above* and on *page 74*.

INGREDIENTS
- 1¼ cups dry green or brown lentils
- ¼ cup dried minced onion
- ¼ cup dried green sweet pepper
- 1 teaspoon salt
- 1 teaspoon dried thyme, crushed
- ½ teaspoon fennel seed, crushed
- ¼ teaspoon crushed red pepper

INSTRUCTIONS
1. Combine all the ingredients. Place in an airtight container or in a self-sealing plastic bag. Store in a cool, dry place for up to 1 year.
2. To prepare, bring 6 cups water to boiling in saucepan. Add dry mix; reduce heat. Simmer, covered, 35 to 40 minutes or until lentils are soft. To serve, ladle stew into bowls. Makes 4 main-dish servings.
Note: Include recipe on a gift tag with the farmer's market stockpot. ❤

olive breadsticks

Shown *left* and on *page 74*.

INGREDIENTS
- 2 cups all-purpose flour
- 2 teaspoons baking powder
- 1 teaspoon salt
- ¼ cup shortening
- ¼ cup black olives, pitted and finely chopped
- ¾ cup milk

INSTRUCTIONS
1. Stir together flour, baking powder, and salt in a medium mixing bowl. Cut in shortening with a pastry cutter or fork until mixture resembles coarse crumbs. Stir in olives. Make a well in the center of the dry mixture, and add milk all at once. Stir with a fork until mixture is just moistened.
2. Turn dough out onto a lightly floured surface. Quickly knead, by gently folding and pressing the dough 10 to 12 strokes or until it is nearly smooth.
3. Roll out dough to a 16×8-inch rectangle, and cut lengthwise into thirty-two ½-inch-wide strips. For each breadstick, twist two strips together. Place on an ungreased baking sheet. Bake in a 450°F oven for 10 minutes or until golden. Serve warm. Makes 16. ❤

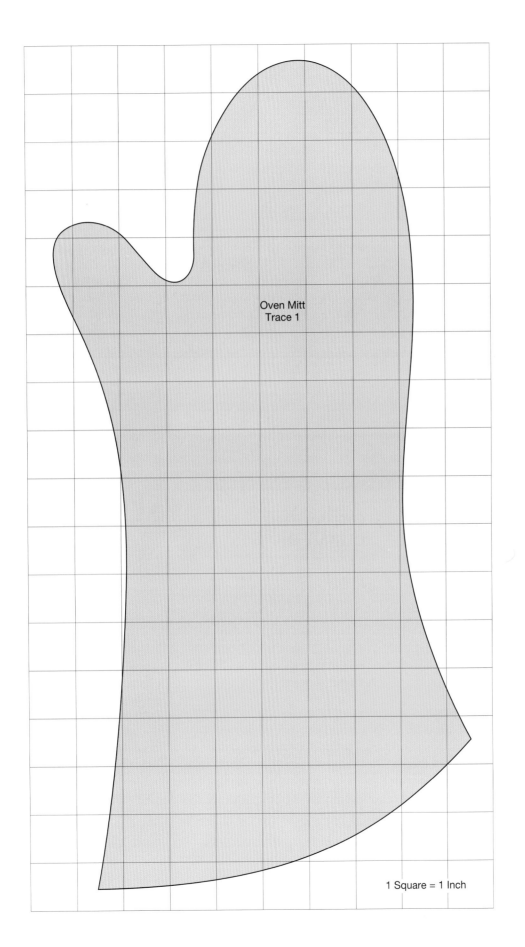

Oven Mitt
Trace 1

1 Square = 1 Inch

2. In a 3-quart saucepan, combine sugar, vinegar, mustard seed, celery seed, and ground mustard. Heat to boiling. Add squash mixture. Return to boiling; remove from heat. Ladle mixture into 2 clean pint jars. Cool 30 minutes. Cover and refrigerate at least 24 hours before serving. Store in refrigerator for up to 1 month. Makes 2 pints (sixteen ¼-cup servings).❤

picnic basket set

Finished size varies.
Shown *above* and on *page 77.*

MATERIALS

- Purchased picnic basket with lid
- Red-and-white check tablecloth
- Coordinating plastic picnic plates
- 12–15 decorative ladybugs
- Crafts glue

INSTRUCTIONS

1. Position the miniature ladybugs around the edge of the basket lid and glue in place.

2. Arrange the tablecloth in the basket as a liner. Put in plastic plates, napkins and napkin rings, and a jar or two of Refrigerator Squash Pickles and a plate of Chocolate Revel Bars.❤

refrigerator squash pickles

Shown *above* and on *page 77.*

INGREDIENTS

- 3 small yellow summer squash, sliced ½ inch thick (about 3 cups)
- ½ cup chopped onion (1 medium)
- 1 large red sweet pepper, cut into ¼-inch-wide strips
- 1 tablespoon salt
- 1 cup sugar
- ¾ cup white vinegar
- ¾ teaspoon mustard seed
- ¾ teaspoon celery seed
- ¼ teaspoon ground mustard

INSTRUCTIONS

1. In a large nonmetal bowl, combine squash, onion, and sweet pepper. Sprinkle salt over vegetables; stir to combine. Cover and refrigerate for 1 hour. Drain off liquid.

chocolate revel bars

Shown *above* and on *page 77.*

INGREDIENTS

- 1 cup butter or margarine
- 2 cups packed brown sugar
- 1 teaspoon baking soda
- 2 eggs
- 2 teaspoons vanilla
- 2½ cups all-purpose flour
- 3 cups quick-cooking rolled oats
- 1½ cups semisweet chocolate pieces
- 1 14-ounce can (1¼ cups) sweetened condensed milk or low-fat sweetened condensed milk
- ½ cup chopped walnuts or pecans
- 2 teaspoons vanilla

INSTRUCTIONS

1. Set aside 2 tablespoons of the butter or margarine. In a large mixing bowl beat the remaining butter or margarine with an electric mixer on medium to high speed for 30 seconds. Add the brown sugar and baking soda. Beat until combined, scraping sides of bowl occasionally. Beat in eggs and 2 teaspoons vanilla until combined. Beat in as much of the flour as you can with the mixer. Stir in remaining flour. Stir in the rolled oats.

2. For filling, in a medium saucepan, combine the reserved 2 tablespoons butter or margarine, chocolate pieces, and sweetened condensed milk. Cook over low heat until chocolate melts, stirring occasionally. Remove from heat. Stir in the walnuts or pecans and the 2 teaspoons vanilla.

3. Press two-thirds (about 3⅓ cups) of the rolled oats mixture into the bottom of an ungreased 15×10×1-inch baking pan. Spread filling evenly over the oat mixture. Dot remaining rolled oats mixture on filling.

4. Bake in a 350°F oven for about 25 minutes or until top is lightly browned (chocolate filling will still look moist). Cool on a wire rack. Cut into bars. Makes 60 bars. ❤

~One More Idea~

napkin rings

Finished size varies.
Shown *above* and on *page 76*.

MATERIALS
- Red and blue print handkerchiefs
- Wooden napkin rings
- Red, blue, yellow, and white acrylic paint
- Spray acrylic sealer
- Decorative butterflies from a crafts store
- Crafts glue

INSTRUCTIONS

1. Paint the wooden napkins rings with red, blue or yellow acrylic paint and allow to dry.

2. Glue butterflies to the wooden napkin rings and allow to dry thoroughly. Spray with a coat of acrylic sealer.

3. Gather the handkerchief corners together. Pull the center handkerchief through the ring. ❤

heart cookie boxes

Finished size varies.
Shown *above* and on *page 78*.

MATERIALS

- Papier-mâché heart-shape box
- Red, blue, and yellow acrylic paint
- Spray acrylic sealer
- Fine-point permanent black marking pen
- Decorated heart-shape sugar cookies
- Bright color cloth napkin

INSTRUCTIONS

1. Paint the heart-shape box with red, blue, or yellow acrylic paint and allow to dry. Spray on a coat of acrylic sealer and allow to dry.

2. Use the black marking pen to write messages of friendship on the box top and sides. Let the ink dry and spray the box with another coat of acrylic sealer.

3. Line the box with a napkin. Fill with an assortment of brightly colored red, blue, and yellow heart-shape cookies.❤

painted cutout cookies

Shown *above* and on *page 78*.

INGREDIENTS

- 1 cup butter
- 1½ cups sugar
- 2 eggs
- 1 teaspoon vanilla
- 3 cups all-purpose flour
- 1 teaspoon baking powder
- ½ teaspoon salt
- ½ teaspoon ground nutmeg
- One recipe Paintbrush Icing (opposite)

INSTRUCTIONS

1. In a medium saucepan, melt butter. Stir in sugar. Remove from heat. Cool for 15 minutes.

2. With a spoon, beat in eggs and vanilla. Place in a large bowl. Stir in flour, baking powder, salt, and nutmeg. Cover surface with clear plastic wrap. Chill in the refrigerator for about 4 hours or until easy to handle.

3. On a floured surface, roll half of dough to ⅛–¼" thickness. Cut into shapes with cookie cutters. Place on an ungreased cookie sheet. Bake in a 375°F oven for 6 to 8 minutes or until edges are very lightly browned. Cool cookies on a wire rack.

4. Frost with Paintbrush Icing. Makes about 60 (3") cookies.❤

paintbrush icing

Shown *opposite, below,* and on *page 78.*

INGREDIENTS
- 4 cups sifted powdered sugar
- 3 tablespoons meringue powder*
- 1/3 cup water
- 1/4 teaspoon lemon extract
- Liquid or paste food coloring

INSTRUCTIONS

1. In a medium bowl, combine the 4 cups sifted powdered sugar and 3 tablespoons meringue powder.*

2. Beating with an electric mixer on low speed, gradually add 1/3 cup water. Beat on high speed for 2 to 3 minutes or until icing becomes thick. Beat in 1/4 teaspoon lemon extract.

3. Divide icing into smaller portions for different colors. Tint icing with paste or liquid food coloring. (Keep icings covered with plastic wrap to prevent drying out.) Thin colored icings with water to the consistency of thick syrup.

4. Spoon a small amount of icing onto a cookie. Spread icing with a metal spatula or use clean artist's paintbrushes to paint it onto the cookies in the desired design.

Note: Look for meringue powder at stores that sell cake-decorating supplies.❤

heart gift tags

Shown *above* and on *page 79.*

MATERIALS
- Small wooden hearts
- Red, blue, yellow, and white acrylic paints
- Spray acrylic sealer
- Small paintbrush
- Decorative ribbon
- Drill and drill bit

INSTRUCTIONS

1. Paint the wooden hearts with red, blue, or yellow acrylic paint and allow to dry.

2. Use white acrylic paint and small paintbrush to add accents.

3. Let dry and spray with coat of acrylic sealer.

4. Drill a small hole, and thread a ribbon through to hang.❤

kid's garden tote
page 104

GIFTS FROM THE
garden

$\mathcal{C}$ultivate a $\mathcal{C}$hild's early interest in gardening with a kid-size garden tote and tools. Include packets of seeds, a miniature watering can, and a journal for recording plantings and progress.

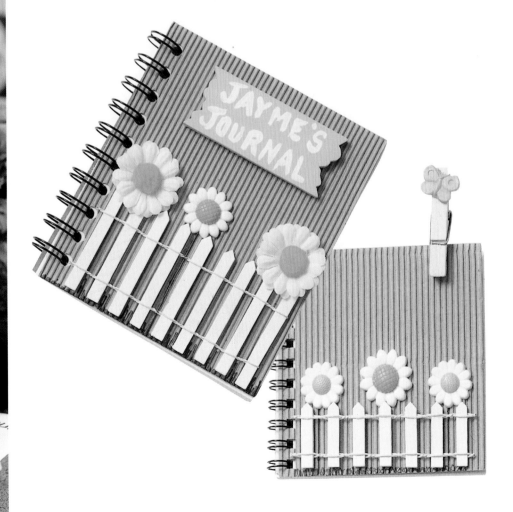

watering can planter

The kitchen-window herb gardener will plant in style with a gift of painted watering cans. Coordinate clever picket-fence journals with the yellow galvanized cans.

**watering can planter
page 105**

seed packet bouquet

Give a gift that keeps on growing with a planter of blooming pansies and spring flower seed packets on sticks. For more color and interest, paint a border of florals to dress up a plain wooden box.

seed packet bouquet
page 106

garden candles

$\mathcal{L}$ooking as if they were fresh-picked from the garden, these candles will bloom indefinitely. For trims, glue artificial ladybugs, leaves, or buttons to the sides of the candles; then dip the candles in melted wax for a soft, double-dipped effect. Paint stems and leaves on the button flowers using candle paints.

**garden candles
page 108**

flowers under glass

Handcrafted glass coasters bring the garden's perfections indoors. For flowers under glass, arrange dried and pressed buds and blooms between two squares of glass secured with a strip of copper foil edging.

**flowers under glass
page 108**

heart wreath
page 109

heart wreath

*T*his versatile wreath will be welcome in almost any style of decorating—from the heart of country to contemporary. Begin with a base of dried German statice, and add annual statice and other dried florals as desired.

blooms in a box

$\mathcal{T}$ransform ordinary wooden eggs into floral masterpieces with something as simple as rice paper or sheer cocktail napkins. Coat the napkin-wrapped egg with a decoupage medium and watch the egg take on a look of its own. For more old-world elegance, cover a wooden tray in the same manner.

blooms in a box
page 110

bunny buddies
page 111

bunny buddies

These bunny buddies are sure to hop out of Mr. MacGregor's garden right into the hearts of kids everywhere. To celebrate Easter or for an early spring treat, give them by the jarful along with eggs and candy.

kid's garden tote

Finished size varies.
Shown *left* and on *page 90*.

MATERIALS
- Small purchased canvas tote bag with side pockets
- Small hand garden tools such as a trowel and a rake
- 12–15 flower buttons, pins, or miniatures
- Permanent marking pens
- Crafts glue

INSTRUCTIONS
1. Glue a row of flower buttons on the pockets of the tote bag, positioning some higher than others. Allow to dry thoroughly.

2. With a permanent marking pen, draw stems and leaves for each flower.

3. At the bottom of the tote, glue a ladybug button and write "How Does Your Garden Grow?" with a permanent marker.

4. Insert small garden tools in the pockets.❤

kid's garden journal

Finished size varies.

Shown *above* and on *page 91*.

MATERIALS

- Small spiral notebook
- Section of miniature picket fence from a crafts store
- Crafts glue
- Precut wood piece for label from a crafts store
- Yellow and white acrylic paints
- Small paintbrush
- Miniature clothespin and butterfly
- Silk or flower miniatures

INSTRUCTIONS

1. Glue picket fence along the lower front portion of the notebook. Glue flowers to the top of the fence posts.

2. Paint the wood piece yellow and allow to dry thoroughly.

3. Carefully center and letter a name on the wood piece using the small paintbrush and white paint. Glue the label on the notebook.

4. Glue a butterfly to the top of the clothes pin to use for a page marker. ❤

~One More Idea~

watering can planter

Finished size varies.

Shown *above* and on *page 92*.

MATERIALS

- Small galvanized watering can
- Light yellow acrylic paint
- Paintbrush
- Vinegar
- Potting soil and gravel
- Herb plant

INSTRUCTIONS

1. Wipe the galvanized watering can with vinegar to help the paint adhere.

2. Paint a stripe around the outer center of the can and around the spout. Let the paint dry.

3. Fill the planter with about 1" of gravel for drainage. Fill to within 1" of the top with potting soil.

4. Plant a herb in it. ❤

seed packet bouquet

Finished size varies.
Shown *above* and on *page 93*.

MATERIALS

- Wooden box with handle
- Acrylic paint: light green, yellow, brown, and white
- Green, light yellow, or white permanent markers
- Paintbrush
- Wooden flower cutouts, in two sizes
- Wooden birdhouse cutout
- Crafts sticks
- Crafts glue
- Seed packets
- Spanish moss
- Potted flowers

INSTRUCTIONS

1. Paint the box and wood of the handle light green. Allow paint to dry.

2. Referring to the example in Diagram 1, *opposite*, draw flower stems and leaves with the green permanent marker. Use the tip of the marker to fill in areas between stems and leaves, as shown in Diagram 2.

3. Paint a brown birdhouse post, referring to Diagram 2.

4. Paint the wooden flower cutouts yellow. Let dry. Using the light yellow or white permanent marker, add lines from the center out. Paint flower centers with a dot of brown.

5. Paint the wooden birdhouse cutout white. Let dry. Using the green permanent marker, make stripes for both sides of the roof and a heart shape for the door.

6. Referring to the photo, glue the flowers and the birdhouse onto the box.

7. Fill the planter with soil and flowers. Cover the soil with Spanish moss.

8. Glue a crafts stick to the back of each seed packet and arrange a seed packet bouquet among the blooms. ❤

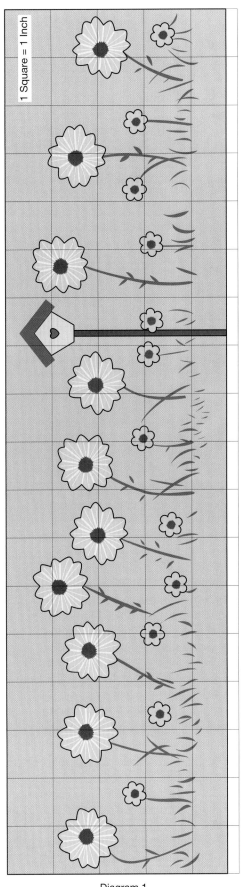

1 Square = 1 Inch

Diagram 1

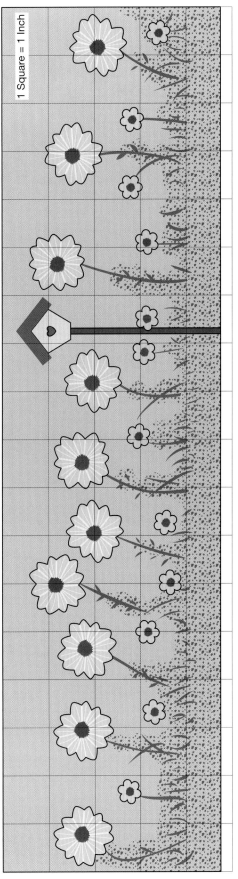

1 Square = 1 Inch

Diagram 2

flowers under glass

Finished size 3x3".

Shown *above* and on *pages 96–97.*

MATERIALS

- Small garden flowers such as pansies or violets, ferns, and leaves
- Paper towels
- Several heavy books
- Two pieces of 3" square double-strength glass for each coaster
- Copper foil edging
- Sheer decorative ribbon

INSTRUCTIONS

1. Place small flowers and leaves on paper towels and carefully place them between the pages of a heavy book. Stack several books on top and allow to dry for about a week or longer, until they feel dry.

2. Carefully arrange flowers and greens on one of the glass squares. Place the second piece of glass over the flowers and greens.

3. Apply copper foil edging to the coasters, following the manufacturer's instructions.

4. For a special touch, stack several coasters and tie them together with a decorative ribbon. ❤

garden candles

Finished size varies.

Shown *above* and on *page 94.*

MATERIALS

- Purchased 3" diameter candles of varying heights
- Clear candle wax from a crafts store
- Dried florals and greens
- Plastic flowers, buttons, and ladybugs
- Candle paints in shades of green
- Crafts glue
- Kitchen tongs
- Aluminum foil
- Aluminum melting pot

INSTRUCTIONS

1. Lightly glue the dried flowers, greens, flower buttons, and ladybugs around the candle. Allow the glue to dry.

2. In the aluminum melting pot, heat the candle wax, following the manufacturer's instructions. Grip the candle at the base with the kitchen tongs and carefully dip the candle into the melted wax until it is completely covered. Remove and place on aluminum foil to dry.

3. Carefully smooth the marks from the tongs with your fingers as the wax begins to cool.

4. When the candle is completely cooled, paint stems and leaves at the base of the flower buttons. ❤

heart wreath

Finished size varies.

Shown *above* and on *page 98*.

MATERIALS

- Heart-shape wreath of German statice
- Dried annual statice in assorted colors
- Dried leaves
- Various dried flowers
- Scissors
- Hot-glue gun and hotmelt adhesive

INSTRUCTIONS

1. Divide annual statice into small pieces. Glue randomly into the German statice wreath.

2. Glue various dried flowers and leaves such as those shown, *right*, throughout the wreath.❤

blooms in a box

Finished size varies.

Shown *above* and on *page 100*.

MATERIALS

- Wooden eggs
- Acrylic paints: blue, pink, yellow
- Acrylic decoupage medium
- Sponge make-up wedges for painting
- Acrylic metallic bronze and champagne paints
- Assorted rice paper napkins or 3-ply decorative napkins
- Wood serving tray
- Sandpaper
- Sanding sealer

INSTRUCTIONS

1. Lightly sand the wooden eggs. Seal eggs with sanding sealer.

2. Paint eggs with blue, pink, or yellow acrylic.

3. Cut floral motifs from napkins. If you use 3-ply napkins, separate layers and use only the printed side.

4. Sponge the eggs with a small amount of decoupage medium. Smooth the napkins around the eggs with your fingers.

5. Paint several coats of decoupage medium onto the eggs, allowing the medium to dry thoroughly after each coat.

6. Buff finish with a dry brush and metallic paint.

7. Follow steps 1–6 to paint and coat the serving tray.❤

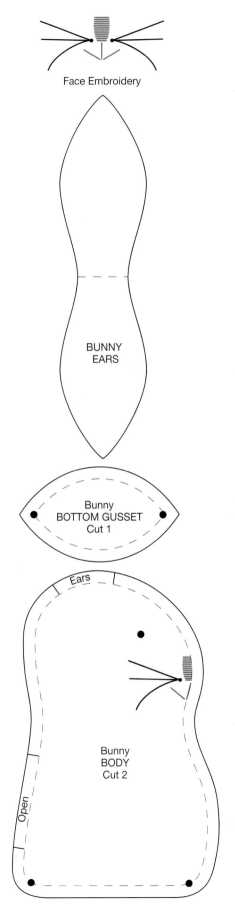

Face Embroidery

BUNNY EARS

Bunny
BOTTOM GUSSET
Cut 1

Ears

Bunny
BODY
Cut 2

Open

bunny buddies

Finished size 3½" tall.

Shown *above* and on *page 102.*

MATERIALS

for each bunny

- 6x6" piece white wool felt
- 2x5" piece colored Ultrasuede
- Pink embroidery floss
- Black buttonhole twist or carpet thread
- Cotton stuffing
- 3 pennies
- 9" of ⅛" satin ribbon
- White pom-pom for tail

INSTRUCTIONS

1. Transfer patterns, *right,* onto tracing paper; cut out.

2. Trace ears, body, and gusset onto white wool felt, referring to the patterns for number of pieces to cut; cut out.

3. Trace Bunny Ears onto Ultrasuede; cut out.

4. Use ⅛" seam allowance unless otherwise directed. Stitch Ultrasuede ears to wool felt ears. Cut at dashed line on the wool felt.

5. Stitch body pieces and gusset together, leaving openings as shown for ears and tails.

6. Turn bunny right side out through tail opening. Place three pennies on gusset (for weight) inside bunny body. Fill bunny with cotton stuffing.

7. Insert ears and tail in openings; hand-stitch to secure.

8. Add embroidery details to face. Tie a ribbon into a bow around the bunny neck.♥

fiesta salsa and chips
page 120

GIFTS OF
ratitude

Expressing Gratitude can be as easy as picking up the phone, mailing a note of thanks, or giving something you've made. Take-along gifts include the fiesta salsa and chips, complete with serving bowls and box, and bright tissue-wrapped muffins tucked into interesting mugs.

festive mugs & muffins
page 121

teacher's tote and notes

Brighten a teacher's day with gifts that are as attractive as they are useful. For a gift to a noteworthy teacher, paint a plain wooden box. Add an apple punch-out border to match note pads and a pencil cup. Make teacher's lunchtime a special occasion with a pocketed lunch tote and a coordinating napkin.

teacher's tote
and notes
page 122

comfort quilt & pillow
page 124

comfort quilt & pillow

*W*hat friend doesn't need a little comforting now and then? Show how much you care by giving a one-patch quilt and pillow. Arrange the ticking stripe center blocks to resemble woven ribbons and toss in a button-embellished pillow. At the window, let your love shine through with sun catchers that frame sentiments of good cheer.

hearts & flowers

**hearts & flowers
sun catchers
page 125**

Fill a keepsake box lined with handmade paper with votive candles to reflect how much you care. Top it off with a painted reminder that "Friendship warms the Heart," and tie it all together with matching ribbon.

friendship candles

friendship candles
page 126

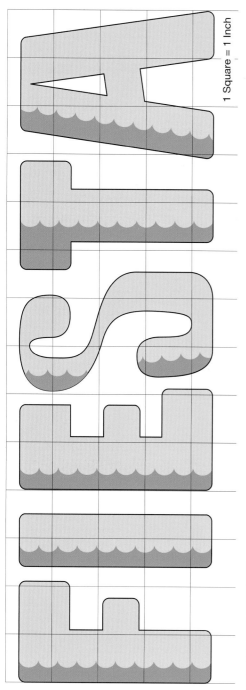

1 Square = 1 Inch

fiesta box

Finished size varies.

Shown *above* and on *page 112*.

MATERIALS

- Wooden box with handles
- Small crockery bowl
- Small canning jar with lid and ring
- Permanent enamel paints: red, yellow, and teal
- 8" circle of cotton fabric for jar top
- Raffia
- Salsa
- Tortilla Crisps
- Ceramic bowl

INSTRUCTIONS

1. Paint the wooden box red. Let the paint dry thoroughly.

2. Using the lettering guide, *left*, draw letters to spell "FIESTA." Paint the letters yellow and teal. Let the paint dry.

3. Using the lettering guide, *below*, paint "Salsa" and red peppers on the side of the small crockery bowl. Let the paint dry.

4. Fill the canning jar with Salsa (see recipe, *opposite*). Top it with the lid. Center the fabric on the lid and seal it with the ring. Tie a raffia bow around the fabric.

5. Arrange the chip bowl, jar of salsa, salsa bowl, and chips in the Fiesta Box. ♥

salsa

INGREDIENTS

- 2—14½-ounce cans chunky pasta-style tomatoes
- 1—4-ounce can diced green chili peppers
- ¼ cup thinly sliced green onions
- ¼ cup snipped cilantro or parsley
- 2 tablespoons lemon juice
- ⅛ teaspoon pepper
- 1 clove garlic, minced
- ¼ teaspoon salt
- 1 recipe Tortilla Crisps (see below)

INSTRUCTIONS

1. Drain tomatoes, reserving ⅓ cup juice; discard remaining juice.

2. Combine tomatoes and reserved juice, chili peppers, green onions, cilantro or parsley, lemon juice, pepper, garlic, and ¼ teaspoon salt. Cover and chill at least 4 hours before serving. Cover and chill leftovers up to 2 weeks. Makes about 2¾ cups salsa.

3. Serve with Tortilla Crisps.

Note: For gift giving, include instructions to keep refrigerated.♥

tortilla crisps

INGREDIENTS

- 12—7" or 8" flour tortillas

INSTRUCTIONS

1. Cut each tortilla into 8 wedges. Spread one-third of the wedges in a 15×10×1" baking pan. Bake in a 350°F oven 5 to 10 minutes or until dry and crisp. Repeat with remaining wedges; cool. Store in an airtight container at room temperature for up to 4 days or in the freezer for up to 3 weeks. Makes 96 crisps (24 appetizer servings).♥

festive mugs & muffins

Shown *above* and on *page 113.*

MATERIALS

- Purchased coffee or latte mugs
- Bright-colored tissue paper
- One recipe Pumpkin-Nut Muffins *(see below)*

INSTRUCTIONS

1. Prepare the Pumpkin-Nut Muffins.

2. Place a sheet of tissue paper in each mug to extend from the mug.

3. Place a muffin, or several if they will fit, into each mug.♥

pumpkin-nut muffins

INGREDIENTS

- 2⅔ cups sifted cake flour or 2⅓ cups unsifted all-purpose flour
- 2 teaspoons baking powder
- 2 teaspoons pumpkin pie spice
- ¼ teaspoon salt
- 2 slightly beaten eggs
- 1¼ cups sugar
- 1¼ cups canned pumpkin
- ⅔ cup cooking oil
- ⅓ cup milk
- ¾ cup chopped walnuts
- ¾ cup light raisins

INSTRUCTIONS

1. Line 2½" (regular) or 1¾" (mini) muffin pans with paper bake cups. Set aside.

2. In a large bowl, stir together flour, baking powder, pumpkin pie spice, and salt. Make a well in center.

3. In another bowl, mix eggs, sugar, pumpkin, cooking oil, and milk. Add to flour mixture. Stir until combined. Fold in walnuts and raisins.

4. Fill prepared pans about ⅔ full with batter. Bake in a 375°F oven for 20 to 25 minutes or until golden for 2½" muffins or for 12 to 15 minutes for 1¾" muffins. Remove from pans; serve warm. Makes 18 regular-size muffins or 72 mini-muffins.♥

teacher's notes

Finished size varies.
Shown *above* and on *page 115.*

MATERIALS

- Wooden box from a crafts store
- Bright-yellow acrylic paint
- Spray acrylic varnish
- Apple paper punch
- Card stock in lime, hot pink, and purple
- Crafts glue
- Sticky notepads in matching shades of lime, hot pink, and purple

INSTRUCTIONS

1. Paint the wooden box with the bright yellow acrylic paint. Let the paint dry.

2. Spray with acrylic varnish and allow to dry thoroughly.

3. Using the apple paper punch, punch out several apples in all three colors. Glue the apple punches to the box edges.

4. Stack notepads on the shelf.❤

teacher's pencil cup

Finished size varies.
Shown *above* and on *page 115.*

MATERIALS

- Soup can with label removed
- Crafting paper
- Spray-mount adhesive
- Bright-yellow acrylic paint
- Spray acrylic varnish
- Pencils

INSTRUCTIONS

1. Paint the can with the bright-yellow acrylic paint. Let the paint dry.

2. Spray the can with acrylic varnish and allow to dry thoroughly.

3. Cut paper to fit the can, allowing ¼" for overlap on the circumference. Spray-mount to can.

4. Fill can with pencils.❤

teacher's lunch tote

Finished size varies.

Shown *above* and on *pages 114–115*.

MATERIALS

Choose heavy cotton in contrasting bright fabrics for each piece.

For the tote
- ¼ yard for center piece
- ¼ yard for side panels
- ¼ yard for pocket
- ⅔ yard lining fabric
- ½ yard 1" decorative ribbon trim for pocket
- 1 yard 1" decorative ribbon trim for tote top edge
- 6 coordinating buttons

For the napkin
- 2—½-yard pieces of contrasting fabric

INSTRUCTIONS

1. *To make the tote,* cut fabrics as shown in the diagram, right.

2. Fold decorative ribbon over the short edges of pocket piece and stitch in place.

3. Right sides up, center the pocket on the center piece. Baste the sides.

4. Right sides together and using a ¼" seam allowance, stitch the side panels to center piece, matching the dots.

5. Sew lining side panels to lining center piece. Press.

6. Wrong sides together, position lining inside of tote.

7. Sew decorative ribbon trim over the top raw edges of the tote. Hand-sew decorative buttons along the top edge of pocket.

8. *To make napkin,* place two 16½" squares right sides together, and stitch around the edges, leaving a 4" opening for turning.

9. Turn right side out and press. Sew opening closed and topstitch ¼" from edges. ❤

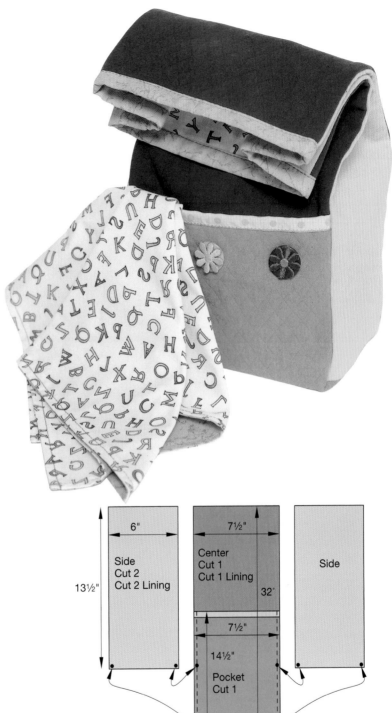

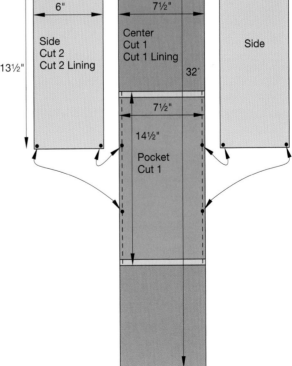

Teacher's Lunch Tote Diagram

comfort quilt

Finished sizes 62×78".

Shown *right* and on *page 116*.

MATERIALS

- 2¾ yards ticking stripe fabric
- ⅓ yard brown fabric with small print
- 1¾ yards rust print fabric
- ½ yard brown fabric with large print
- 3¾ yards backing fabric
- 66x82" piece of quilt batting
- Heavy cotton thread for tying
- Large embroidery needle

Cut the following pieces from the ticking stripe fabric
- 165—4½" squares for quilt center

Cut the following pieces from the brown fabric with small print
- 7—1½x42" strips for inner border

Cut the following pieces from the rust print fabric
- 7—8½x42" strips for outer border

Cut the following pieces from the brown fabric with large print
- 4—8½" squares for corners

Quantities specified are for 44/45"-wide 100% cotton fabrics. All measurements include a ¼" seam allowance.

INSTRUCTIONS

1. Alternating the stripe direction, sew the 4½" squares together into fifteen rows with eleven squares in each row. Alternate the direction of the squares in each row. Sew the rows together (see Diagram 1).

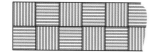

Diagram 1

2. Cut one 42" inner border strip in half. Join each half to a 42" inner border strip. Press. Sew one strip to the bottom and one strip to the top of the quilt. Trim to fit and press the seams toward the borders. Join the remaining inner border strips into two long strips and sew them to the right and left sides of the quilt top. Trim to fit and press the seams toward the borders.

3. Cut one 42" outer border strip in half and join each piece to an outer border strip. Press. Sew one strip to the bottom and one strip to the top. Trim to fit and press the seams toward the borders.

4. Join the remaining outer border strips to make two strips. Measure each side of the quilt top, excluding the top and bottom outer borders. Add ½" seam allowance and cut each border strip to that measurement. Sew two 8½" corner blocks to each border strip. Press. Matching long raw edges, sew the border to the sides of the quilt top. Press the seams toward the border (see Diagram 2).

5. Sew backing pieces together to equal the size of the quilt. Layer backing and quilt top right sides together. Place on top of batting. Stitch around the edge of quilt, leaving about 12" open on one side for turning.

6. Turn right side out, press edges, and hand-stitch the opening closed.

7. Finish quilt by tying in the corners of each square. ♥

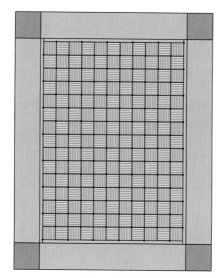

Diagram 2

comfort pillow

Finished sizes 18x18".

Shown *opposite* and on *page 116.*

MATERIALS

- ²/₃ yard brown fabric with large print
- 1¹/₃ yards ticking stripe fabric
- ²/₃ yard rust print fabric
- 25—¾" buttons
- 18"-square fiberfill pillow form

INSTRUCTIONS

1. Cut the brown fabric into a 19" square. Cut the ticking stripe fabric into a 19" square and four 5×42" strips. Cut the rust print fabric into four 4¾×42" strips.

2. Right sides together, sew the ticking strips together along the narrow ends to make a continuous loop. Repeat for the rust print strips. Press seams.

3. Right sides together, sew loops along one edge to make the ruffle. Press in half lengthwise, ¼" away from seam (see Diagram 1).

4. Sew two rows of gathering threads close to the raw edge of the loop. Pull up the threads to fit the

Diagram 1

pillow edges. Matching raw edges, baste the ruffle loop to the pillow top (see Diagram 2).

5. Right sides together, position the ticking square on the pillow top

Diagram 2

(see Diagram 3). Using a ½" seam allowance, stitch around outer edge, leaving an 8" opening on one side. Turn right side out and press.

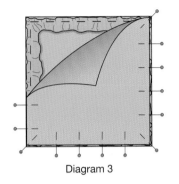

Diagram 3

6. Sew decorative buttons onto pillow top in five rows of five buttons each.

7. Insert a pillow form into opening and hand-stitch the opening closed.❤

hearts & flowers sun catchers

Finished sizes vary.

Shown *above, below,* and on *page 117.*

MATERIALS

- Glass hearts with hanging hole
- Dried flowers
- Decorative stickers
- Rice paper
- Decoupage medium
- Crafts glue
- Copper foil edging
- Sheer decorative ribbon

INSTRUCTIONS

1. Decoupage flowers or stickers faces up onto the back of each glass heart. Allow to dry thoroughly.

2. Trace heart shapes onto rice paper and cut out. Glue paper to the back of the hearts.

3. Apply copper foil edging to the hearts, following the manufacturer's instructions. Lace sheer ribbon through hanging holes.❤

friendship candles

Finished size varies.

Shown *above* and on *pages 118–119*.

MATERIALS

- Wooden, hinged box
- Floral decorator block
- Acrylic paints: cream, sage, dark green, violet, light blue, yellow, and black
- Sponge brush
- Handmade floral paper
- Clear acrylic sealer
- Paintbrush
- Crafts glue
- Votive candles
- Decorative papers
- Sheer decorative ribbon

INSTRUCTIONS

1. Paint the box cream and allow the paint to dry. Follow with a coat of acrylic sealer.

2. Trace the heart pattern and lettering guide, *opposite,* onto the top of the box lid.

3. Paint the heart dark green. Let the paint dry.

4. Paint the lettering in the center of the heart black. Let the paint dry.

5. Referring to photograph, *above,* for color placement, sponge flowers around the heart. Allow to dry. Seal with one or more coats of acrylic sealer, allowing ample drying time after each coat.

6. Cut handmade floral paper to fit the inside of the lid, and glue it in place.

7. Layer sheets of decorative paper in the box. Fill box with votive candles. ❤

Friendship warms the Heart

Life together before...

Happily ever after

Our Wedding

m

**keepsake photo
boxes
page 136**

GIFTS FOR THE
emories

$\mathcal{M}$emories in the $\mathcal{M}$aking are worth storing

beautifully. A trio of boxes will become treasured keepsakes

to hold precious memories for

a newly married couple.

Dress cardboard

boxes in handmade

paper, and add flower-

and bead-decorated

window labels topped

with silk blossoms.

anniversary memory mats

An anniversary celebration is cause for memories and love notes from the family, *below*. At a reception, use a framed photo of the anniversary couple as a guest register, *opposite*. Both memory mats are extrawide to accommodate written messages from family and friends.

memory mats
page 137

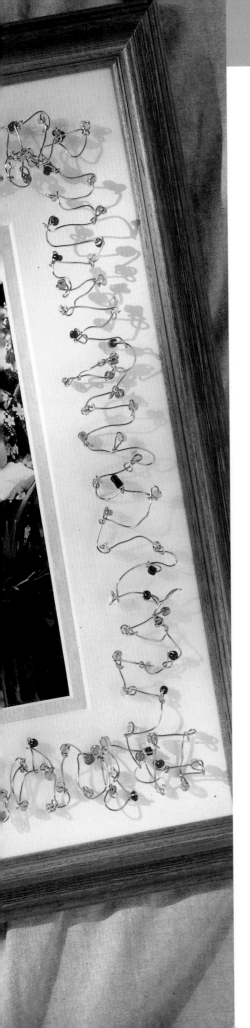

vacation memories

*W*hen the family takes a trip together, make the event more memorable with a frame to match the occasion. Here, memories of a trip to Hawaii are framed with an extrawide mat that holds beads strung on copper wire and bright crafting letters. You may want to handwrite the names and ages of the gathered clan and include the complete date. For more memories of sun, surf, sand, and sailing, add stickers and other appropriate accents.

baby's first frames

One of the great joys
of parenthood is looking
forward to Baby's firsts—
from bath to birthday.
The new arrival's parents
will welcome a gift
basket brimming with
handcrafted paper
frames ready and waiting for those
treasured snapshots.

baby's first frames
page 138

box from the suede paper with the crafts knife. Cut out center of suede shadow box.

5. With the calligraphy pen, write a message on the card stock. Allow to dry.

6. Place a plastic sheet and handwritten card in the center of suede shadow box piece. Fold left and right sides together; fold up the bottom side. Using a small amount of crafts glue, secure sides.

7. Fill shadow box with seed beads. Fold down top side and secure with a small amount of crafts glue. Glue to the front of box and allow to dry.

8. Glue grosgrain ribbon to inside of box to cover raw edge of paper, (see diagram *below*). ❤

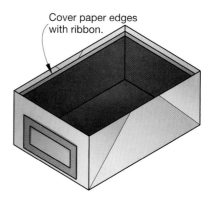

Cover paper edges with ribbon.

keepsake photo boxes

Finished sizes 7½x11x4½".

Shown above on *pages 128–129*.

MATERIALS

- Handmade floral paper
- 1 yard grosgrain ribbon
- 1 sheet suede paper
- 1 5x3" sheet card stock
- 1 5x3" plastic sheet
- Dried flowers and greens
- Coordinating seed beads
- Spraymount adhesive
- Crafts knife
- Crafts glue
- Calligraphy pen

INSTRUCTIONS

1. Measure box sides and bottom and allow for ½" overlap for top of box sides. Cut handmade paper to fit.

2. Repeat Step 1 for lid.

3. Apply spraymount adhesive to back side of sheets. Cover box and lid, folding in sides of paper in envelope fashion.

4. Following the diagram dimensions, *below,* cut out shadow

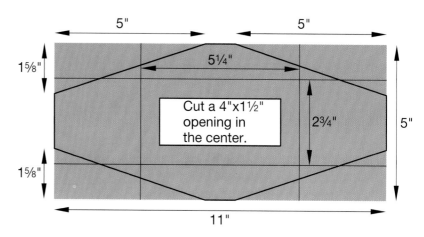

Cut a 4"x1½" opening in the center.

memory mats

Finished size varies.

Shown *above* on *pages 130–133.*

MATERIALS

- Framed photos with 2–3" mat borders for writing or decorating
- Copper wire
- Beads
- Scrapbook alphabet
- Ink pen
- Clear crafts glue

INSTRUCTIONS

1. Have each photo professionally framed with a 2–3" mat border.

2. Using the photos shown here as inspiration, add embellishments, such as personal notes, signatures, scrapbooking letters, stickers, or beads strung on copper wire and twisted to fit the border. ♥

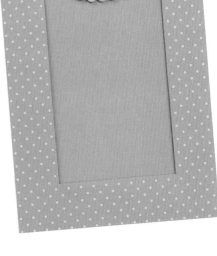

baby's first frames

Finished size 6½x8¼".

Shown *above* and on *pages 134–135.*

MATERIALS

- 6½x8¼" piece of scrapbook paper
- 5¼x7" piece of coordinating scrapbook paper for frame back
- Ruler
- Crafts knife
- Alphabet beads from crafts store
- Embroidery floss
- Soft lead pencil
- Crafts glue
- 3x5" photograph of a baby's first

INSTRUCTIONS

1. Draw a 3x4¾" rectangle in the center of the 6½x8¼" paper (see Diagram 1, *opposite*).

2. Draw a ½" border inside the 3x4¾" rectangle. Connect the corners by drawing diagonal lines (see Diagram 2, *opposite*).

3. Draw a 1¼" border outside the 3x4¾" rectangle (see Diagram 3, *opposite*).

4. Cut out the innermost square using a crafts knife. Trim the outer edges at an angle (see Diagram 4). Using the ruler as a guide, fold back the edges (see Diagram 5, *opposite*).

5. Glue inside folded border (see Diagram 6, *opposite*).

6. Cut a 5¼x7" frame background from scrapbook paper and center on the back. Glue the bottom and one side (see Diagram 7, *opposite*).

7. String a beaded message onto embroidery floss and glue to the top (see Diagram 8, *opposite*).

8. Insert Baby's photo in frame.♥

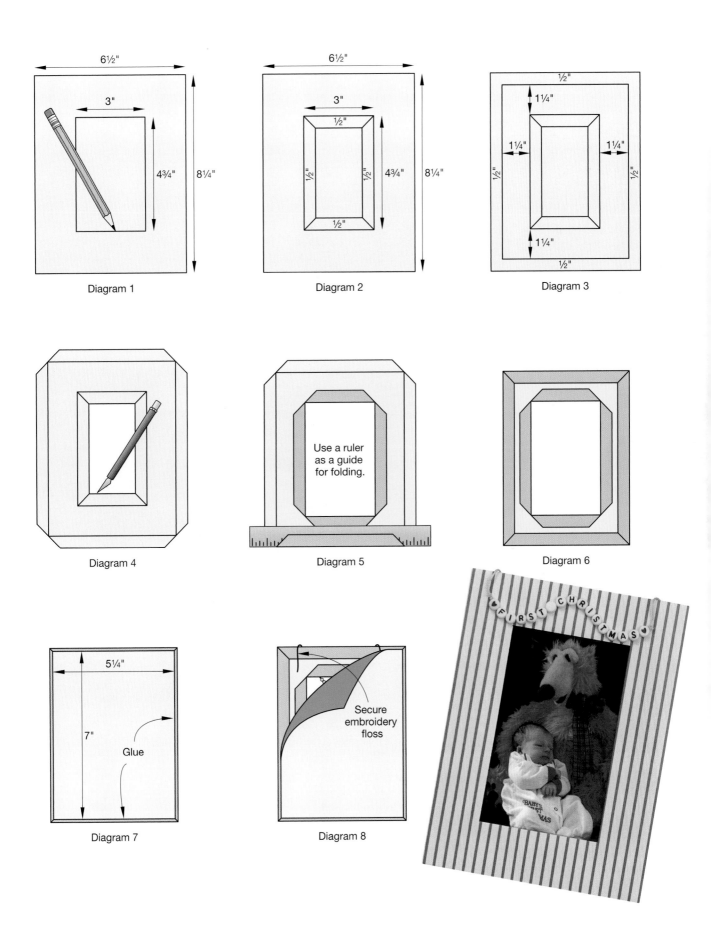

Diagram 1

Diagram 2

Diagram 3

Diagram 4

Use a ruler as a guide for folding.

Diagram 5

Diagram 6

Glue

Diagram 7

Secure embroidery floss

Diagram 8

crazy-quilted
patchwork projects
page 148

GIFTS FOR THE
holidays

*C*razy-quilted *P*atchwork lends an air of old-fashioned ambience to a holiday stocking and a box to hold season's greetings. To decorate the unpainted wooden box, cut cards from Christmases past into irregular shapes. Glue the shapes to the sides of the box and connect them with faux decorative stitching using a pen. For a gift-within-a gift, fill the stocking with brightly wrapped cherry scones.

holiday loaves

**holiday bread wraps
page 150**

*B*read goes beyond basic when dressed for gift

giving in festive red and green holiday wraps that are

quick-stitched from felt and doilies. Recipes for the

Very Cherry Nut Bread, Carrot Quick Bread, and

Blueberry-Orange Bread are on *page 151.*

ruffled pillow and
piping pillow
page 152

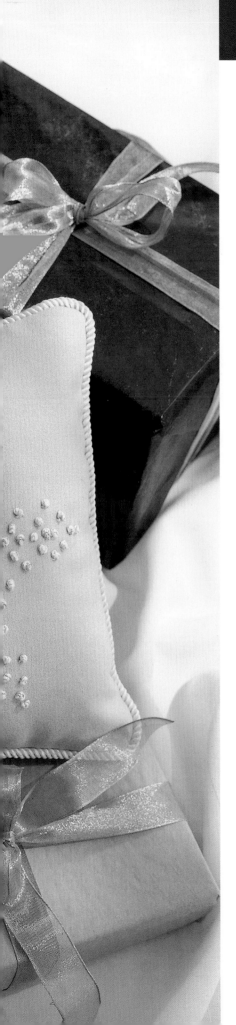

sweet treats & snowflakes

*L*ike the first snowflakes of the season,

these doily-trimmed tins filled with sweet treats,

along with a pair of candlewicking pillows, will

be welcome sights for family and friends.

snow folks

Smiling snow folks made from socks will bring a bit of Christmas cheer to your holiday home. Warm up these frosty characters with a plaid wool cape for the snowlady and a scarf for the snowman. Craft the cute caps using cuffs cut from socks.

**snow folks
page 157**

patchwork stocking

Finished size is 10½x17".

Shown *above* and on *page 140*.

MATERIALS

- Velvet, satin, brocade, taffeta, and other festive fabrics
- 18x9" piece of muslin for patchwork foundation
- ½ yard of velvet or velveteen
- ½ yard of brocade for lining
- Assorted colors of embroidery floss to coordinate with fabrics
- 20" of metallic beaded trim

INSTRUCTIONS

1. Enlarge the cuff pattern using folded graph paper. Cut out and unfold the graph paper. Trace around the pattern on the muslin with an erasable marker. Do not cut out.

2. Lay the muslin on a work surface. Select two fabric pieces that have at least one straight edge each. Pin one piece, right side up, in the center of the muslin (see Diagram 1). Right sides facing, align the straight edge of the second piece with the first. Stitch ¼" along the straight edge. Finger-press the fabric to the right side (see Diagram 2).

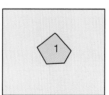

Diagram 1

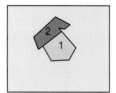

Diagram 2

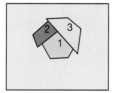

Diagram 3

3. Select a third fabric piece that is long enough to cover one raw edge of the joined pieces. Align it, facedown, along the edge and stitch a ¼" seam allowance. Trim the first two fabrics even with the edge of the third. Finger-press the third piece to the right side (see Diagram 3). Continue adding pieces to cover the muslin cuff.

4. Referring to the stitches shown, *opposite,* add decorative embroidery stitches to the crazy patchwork.

5. Enlarge the stocking pattern using graph paper; cut out. Fold velveteen fabric wrong sides together and cut two stockings. Cut two from lining fabric. With right sides together and using a ¼" seam allowance, sew around the sides and bottom of the stocking, leaving the top open. Turn right sides out and press. Sew together lining pieces but do not turn right sides out. Insert lining into stocking.

6. Lay the cuff pattern the patchwork. Cut along edges of cuff pattern. Use the cuff pattern to cut out a cuff lining.

7. Position and pin beaded trim on the patchwork cuff, selvage edge ¼" from the bottom raw edge. Right sides together, sew cuff lining and patchwork cuff together along the bottom. Sew the seam opposite the fold on the pattern.

8. Turn the cuff right side out and lightly press. Insert the cuff inside the stocking with the right side of the cuff next to the lining and the cuff seam at the center back of the stocking. Pin and stitch around top edge. Turn cuff to the right side and over stocking top. Sew decorative loop to the heel side of the stocking for hanging.❤

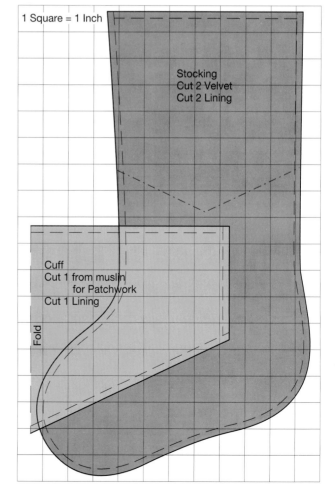

1 Square = 1 Inch

Stocking
Cut 2 Velvet
Cut 2 Lining

Cuff
Cut 1 from muslin
   for Patchwork
Cut 1 Lining

Fold

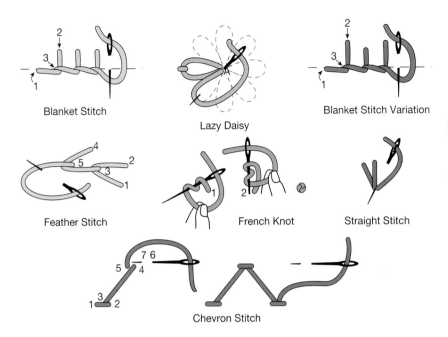

Blanket Stitch

Lazy Daisy

Blanket Stitch Variation

Feather Stitch

French Knot

Straight Stitch

Chevron Stitch

cherry scones

Shown *below* and on *page 140.*

INGREDIENTS

- ½ cup dried sweet cherries or raisins
- 2 cups all-purpose flour
- 3 tablespoons brown sugar
- 2 teaspoons baking powder
- ½ teaspoon baking soda
- ½ teaspoon salt
- ¼ cup margarine or butter
- 1 teaspoon finely shredded orange peel
- 1 8-ounce carton dairy sour cream
- 1 beaten egg yolk
- 1 slightly beaten egg white

INSTRUCTIONS

1. Pour enough boiling water over dried cherries or raisins to cover. Let stand 5 minutes. Drain well.

2. Meanwhile, stir together flour, brown sugar, baking powder, baking soda, and ½ teaspoon salt in a large mixing bowl.

3. Using a pastry blender, cut in margarine or butter until mixture resembles coarse crumbs. Stir in drained cherries and orange peel. Make a well in the center. Stir together sour cream and egg yolk; add all at once to flour mixture. With a fork, stir until combined (mixture may seem dry).

4. Turn dough out onto a lightly floured surface. Quickly knead dough by gently folding and pressing for 10 to 12 strokes or until nearly smooth. Pat or lightly roll dough into a 7" circle. Cut into 12 wedges.

5. Arrange wedges on an ungreased baking sheet about 1" apart. Brush with egg white. Bake in a 400°F oven for 10 to 12 minutes or until light brown. Cool on a wire rack for 10 minutes. Serve warm. Makes 12.❤

sour cream-cherry muffins

Shown *below* and on *page 140.*

INGREDIENTS

- 2 cups all-purpose flour
- ½ cup sugar
- 2 teaspoons baking powder
- ¼ teaspoon salt
- 2 eggs
- ½ cup dairy sour cream
- ½ cup milk
- ¼ cup cooking oil
- ½ teaspoon finely shredded lemon peel
- ¼ teaspoon almond extract
- 1 cup dried tart red cherries, coarsely chopped
- ½ cup chopped almonds
- Lemon Glaze

INSTRUCTIONS

1. Line 12 2½" muffin pans with paper baking cups or 36 1¾" mini-muffin pans with miniature paper baking cups. Set aside.

2. Stir together flour, sugar, baking powder, and salt in a large mixing bowl. Make a well in the center of the dry mixture. In a medium mixing bowl, combine eggs, sour cream, milk, oil, lemon peel, and almond extract; mix well. Add all at once to the dry mixture. Stir just until moistened (batter should be lumpy). Fold in cherries and nuts. Spoon into prepared muffin cups, dividing batter evenly (cups will be full).

3. Bake in a 400°F oven for 15 to 18 minutes for regular muffins, and 12 to 15 minutes for mini-muffins, or until golden brown. Cool in muffin cups on a wire rack for 5 minutes. Remove muffins. Brush lightly with Lemon Glaze. Makes 12 or 36.

4. For gift giving, prepare and bake muffins as directed; cool completely. Do not glaze. Place in a freezer container or bag; freeze for up to 3 months. Before serving or giving as a gift, remove from freezer and thaw at room temperature. Prepare Lemon Glaze; brush muffins lightly with glaze.

Lemon Glaze: Stir together ¾ cup sifted powdered sugar, 2 teaspoons lemon juice, and enough water (2 to 3 teaspoons) to make a thin glaze.❤

patchwork card box

Finished size varies.

Shown *above* and on *page 141*.

MATERIALS

- Wooden card holder
- Red acrylic paint
- Assorted Christmas cards
- Red and green fine-tip marking pens
- Decoupage medium
- Tracing paper
- Crafts scissors
- Crafts glue

INSTRUCTIONS

1. Paint card holder red and allow to dry.

2. Using tracing paper, cover the sides of the box. Draw irregular shapes to divide each side, allowing about ⅛" space between shapes. Number each shape. Cut Christmas cards into pieces using the tracings as a pattern (see Box Diagrams, *below*).

3. Glue pieces lightly in place.

4. With marking pens, draw on decorative "stitching" designs (see Stitching Samples).

5. Add a holiday message cut from a card on the back of the box. Coat the box with decoupage medium. ❤

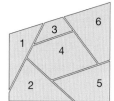

Box Diagrams

Stitching Samples

holiday bread wrap

Finished size is about 14×16".

Shown *above* and on *page 142*.

MATERIALS

- Purchased cotton lace doily, about 12x14"
- Red or green felt, about 4" larger in diameter than doily
- Red, green, and white pearl cotton and coordinating ribbon
- 2 decorative Christmas buttons
- 2 decorative rings for closure
- 1 yard Christmas ribbon

INSTRUCTIONS

1. Place doily on felt and pin in place. Use the scalloped edge of the doily as a guide and cut the felt about ¾" beyond the edge as shown in the Cutting Diagram, *below*.

2. Blanket-stitch around the edges of the felt using embroidery floss.

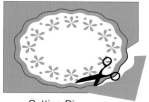

Cutting Diagram

3. Embellish the doily with decorative stitches, such as a row of red and white French knots along the edge (see stitch diagrams on *page 149)*. Make stitches through the doily and the felt.

4. Sew on decorative buttons and ring closures on opposite sides of the inside. Wrap around cellophane-covered holiday breads. Thread Christmas ribbon through the ring closures and tie it into a bow. ❤

very cherry nut bread

Shown *above* and on *page 143.*

INGREDIENTS

- 2½ cups all-purpose flour
- ½ cup granulated sugar
- ½ cup packed brown sugar
- 3½ teaspoons baking powder
- ½ teaspoon salt
- 1 egg
- 1¼ cups milk
- 3 tablespoons cooking oil
- ½ teaspoon almond extract
- 1 10-ounce jar (1 cup) maraschino cherries, well drained and coarsely chopped
- ⅔ cup chopped almonds

INSTRUCTIONS

1. Lightly grease a 9×5×3-inch loaf pan and set aside.

2. In a large mixing bowl, stir together flour, granulated sugar, brown sugar, baking powder, and salt. In a small bowl, stir together egg, milk, cooking oil, and almond extract until well combined.

3. Add egg mixture to flour mixture all at once. Stir until just moistened. Fold in the maraschino cherries and chopped almonds. Pour batter into prepared pan.

4. Bake in a 350°F oven about 1 hour or until a wooden toothpick inserted near the center comes out clean. Cool in loaf pan on a wire rack for 10 minutes. Remove from loaf pan. Cool completely on the wire rack. Wrap and store for 8 hours or overnight before slicing. Makes 1 loaf (16 servings).❤

carrot quick bread

Shown *above* and on *page 143.*

INGREDIENTS

- 2½ cups all-purpose flour
- ½ cup toasted wheat germ
- 2 teaspoons baking powder
- 1 teaspoon ground cinnamon or finely shredded lemon peel or finely shredded orange peel (optional)
- ½ teaspoon baking soda
- ½ teaspoon salt
- 3 beaten eggs
- 1 cup granulated sugar
- 2¼ cups finely shredded carrot
- ½ cup packed brown sugar
- ½ cup cooking oil
- ½ cup chopped nuts (optional)

INSTRUCTIONS

1. Grease the bottoms and ½" up the sides of two 8×4×2-inch loaf pans. Set aside. In a large mixing bowl, stir together flour, wheat germ, baking powder, cinnamon or citrus peel, if desired, and the baking soda, and salt. Make a well in the center of the flour mixture.

2. In a medium mixing bowl, combine the eggs, granulated sugar, carrot, brown sugar, and oil; mix well. Add all at once to dry mixture. Stir just until moistened (batter should be lumpy). Stir in nuts, if desired.

3. Divide batter evenly between loaf pans. Bake in a 350°F oven for 45 to 55 minutes or until a wooden toothpick inserted near the center comes out clean. Cool in pans on wire racks for 10 minutes. Remove from pans and cool thoroughly on wire racks. Wrap and store for 8 hours or overnight before slicing. Makes 2 loaves (24 servings).❤

blueberry-orange bread

Shown *above* and on *page 143.*

INGREDIENTS

- 2 cups all-purpose flour
- 1 teaspoon baking powder
- ½ teaspoon salt
- ¼ teaspoon baking soda
- 2 tablespoons butter, cut up
- ¼ cup boiling water
- 1 egg, slightly beaten
- 1 cup sugar
- ½ cup orange juice
- 1 cup fresh blueberries

INSTRUCTIONS

1. Grease the bottom and ½-inch up the sides of an 8×4×2-inch loaf pan; set aside.

2. In a large bowl, stir together flour, baking powder, salt, and baking soda; make a well in center and set aside. Stir together butter and boiling water until butter is melted. In a medium bowl, combine egg, sugar, and orange juice; stir in the butter mixture. Add to the dry ingredients, stirring just until moistened. Fold in blueberries. Spoon batter into the prepared pan.

3. Bake in a 350°F oven about 60 minutes or until a toothpick inserted near the center comes out clean. Cool 10 minutes. Remove loaf from pan. Cool completely on a wire rack. Wrap in foil and store overnight. Makes 1 loaf (16 slices).❤

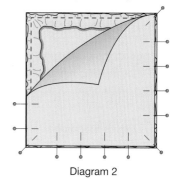

Diagram 2

Note: To insert cording on the ruffled pillow, see Step 3 for Piping Pillow, and insert it before attaching the ruffle.

6. Right sides together, position the 19" white satin or taffeta square on the pillow top (see Diagram 2). Using a ½" seam allowance, stitch around outer edge, leaving an

8" opening on one side. Turn right side out and press.

7. Insert a pillow form into the opening; hand-stitch to close. ♥

ruffled pillow

Finished size is 18" square.
Shown *above* and on *page 144.*

MATERIALS

- ⅔ yard antique white wool or wool blend fabric
- 1⅔ yards antique white satin or taffeta fabric
- Cream pearl cotton floss and silver metallic floss
- Embroidery needle with large eye
- 2 yards of antique white decorative cording (optional)
- 18" square fiberfill pillow form
- Air-soluble pen

INSTRUCTIONS

1. Cut the antique white wool fabric into a 19" square.

2. Transfer snowflake patterns, *opposite,* randomly (see diagram for placement on *page 154*) on the pillow top using the air-soluble pen. Using a strand of pearl cotton and

metallic floss together, make French knots as shown on the patterns.

3. Cut the antique white satin or taffeta fabric into a 19" square and four 5×42" strips.

4. Right sides together, sew the white satin or taffeta strips together on the narrow ends to make a continuous strip. Press seams.

5. Sew two rows of gathering threads close to the raw edge of the strip. Pull up threads to fit the pillow. Matching raw edges, baste the ruffle to the pillow top (see Diagram 1). Include optional cording for piping, if desired.

Diagram 1

piping pillow

Finished size is 10" square
Shown *above* and on *pages 144.*

MATERIALS

- ½ yard ecru wool or knit fabric
- 1¼ yards of antique white decorative cording
- Cream pearl cotton floss and silver metallic floss
- Embroidery needle with large eye
- 10"-square fiberfill pillow form
- Air-soluble pen

INSTRUCTIONS

1. Cut the ecru wool or knit fabric into two 11" squares.

2. Transfer the large snowflake pattern *(page 154)* to the pillow top using the air-soluble pen.

3. Combining a strand of pearl cotton and metallic floss, make

French knots as shown on the patterns *(pages 153–154)*.

2. Baste cording on right side of pillow back (see Diagram 3). Match right side of pillow top to pillow back. Using a ½" seam allowance, stitch around edges, leaving an 8" opening on one side. Turn right side out and press.

4. Insert pillow into the opening and hand-stitch to close.❤

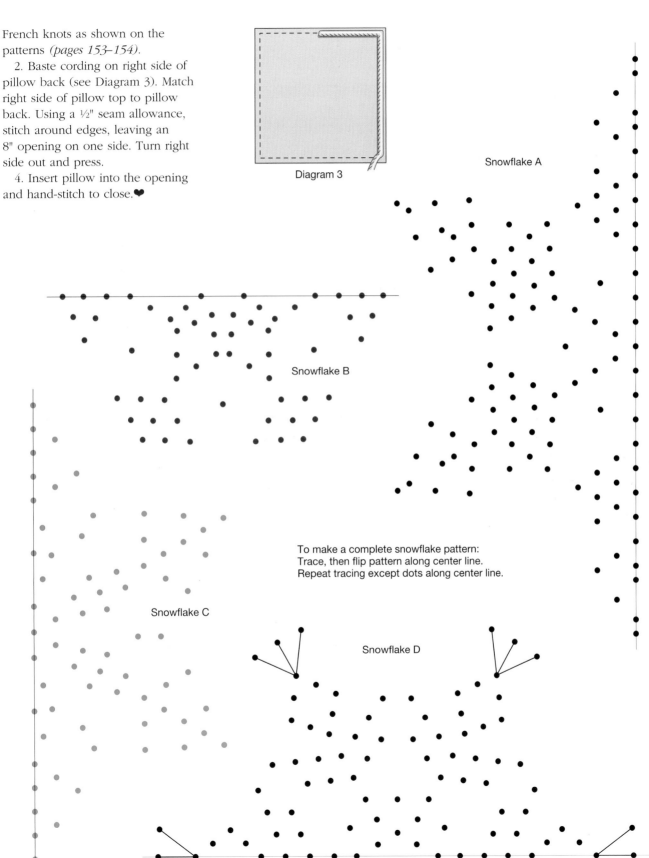

Diagram 3

Snowflake A

Snowflake B

Snowflake C

To make a complete snowflake pattern:
Trace, then flip pattern along center line.
Repeat tracing except dots along center line.

Snowflake D

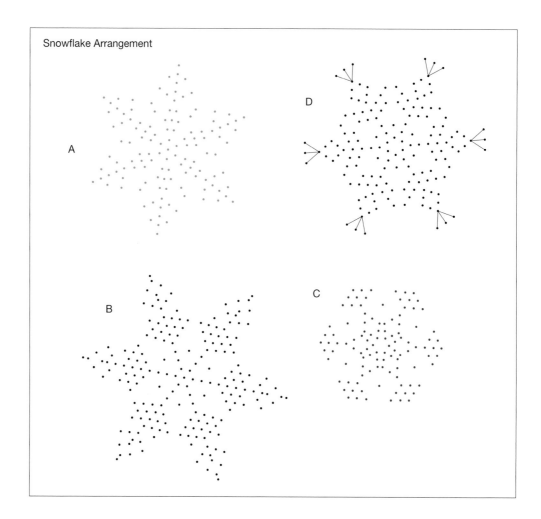

Snowflake Arrangement

A

D

B

C

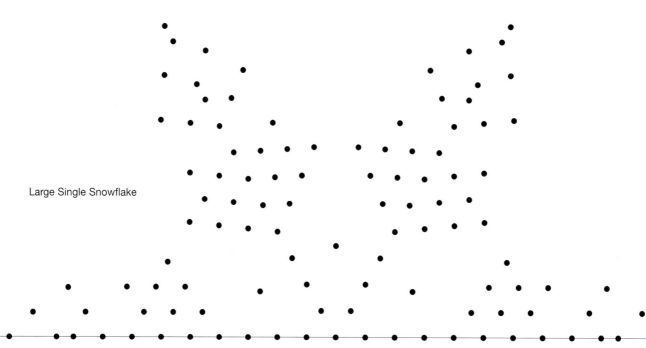

Large Single Snowflake

snowflake tin

Finished size varies.
Shown *above* and on *page 145.*

MATERIALS
- Purchased gold tin
- Lacy paper doily
- Spray-mount adhesive
- Tissue paper
- Sheer decorative ribbon

INSTRUCTIONS
1. Spray back of doily and position on the lid.
2. Line tin with tissue and fill with candy or baked treats.
3. Place lid on the tin securely and tie with a sheer ribbon. Add a handmade gift tag.❤

~One More Idea~

gift tags

Finished size varies.
Shown *right* and on *page 145.*

MATERIALS
- Ready-made gift tags
- Paper doilies
- Crafts glue
- Metallic gold thread

INSTRUCTIONS
1. Cut and glue bits of paper doilies to fit the tops of the Gift Tags.
2. Glue in place.
3. Add thread ties.❤

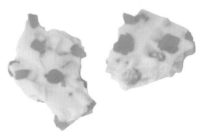

apricot macadamia nut bark

Shown *above* and on *page 145.*

INGREDIENTS
- ¼ cup coarsely chopped macadamia nuts, hazelnuts (filberts), or almonds
- 1 pound white baking pieces
- ⅓ cup finely snipped dried apricots
- 2 tablespoons finely snipped dried apricots

INSTRUCTIONS
1. Toast nuts by spreading them in a single layer in a shallow baking pan. Bake at 350°F for 7 to 9 minutes or until toasted, stirring occasionally. Cool.
2. Meanwhile, line a baking sheet with foil; set aside.
3. Heat baking pieces in a heavy 2-quart saucepan over low heat, stirring constantly until melted and smooth. Remove from heat. Stir in nuts and the ⅓ cup dried apricots.
4. Pour mixture onto the prepared baking sheet, spreading to about a 10" circle. Sprinkle with the 2 tablespoons dried apricots, lightly pressing them into mixture. Chill about 30 minutes or until firm.
5. Use the foil to lift candy from the baking sheet; break candy into pieces. Store candy, tightly covered, in the refrigerator. Makes about 1¼ pounds of candy (40 servings).

Note: For gift giving, include instructions to keep refrigerated.❤

almond-chocolate cups

Shown *below* and on *page 145*.

INGREDIENTS

- 1 3-ounce package cream cheese, softened
- ¼ to ½ teaspoon almond extract
- 3 cups sifted powdered sugar
- ¼ cup finely chopped toasted almonds
- 1 12-ounce package (2 cups) semisweet chocolate pieces
- 16 ounces chocolate-flavored candy coating, cut up
- Small foil candy cups

INSTRUCTIONS

1. Beat cream cheese and almond extract in a medium mixing bowl until smooth. Gradually add powdered sugar, stirring until mixture is thoroughly combined. (If necessary, knead in the last of the powdered sugar by hand.) Stir or knead in chopped almonds.

2. Divide mixture into four equal portions. On a cutting board, roll one portion at a time to a 12" long rope; cut crosswise into ½" pieces. Cover with plastic wrap to prevent drying out as you work with candy.

3. Melt together chocolate pieces and candy coating in a heavy medium saucepan over low heat, stirring just until smooth. Remove from heat. Place foil cups in large shallow pan. Spoon some of the melted chocolate mixture into one-fourth of the candy cups, filling each cup about ⅓ full.

4. Press a piece of cheese mixture in center of each cup (chocolate will not completely cover the cheese mixture). Repeat with remaining filling and chocolate, working with one-fourth at a time. If chocolate starts to set up, reheat over low heat just until smooth. Drizzle any remaining chocolate over white portion of candies, if desired.

5. Set cups aside until firm at room temperature (about 30 minutes) or in refrigerator about 10 minutes. Store in a tightly covered container in the refrigerator. Makes about 96 pieces.

Note: For gift giving, include instructions to keep refrigerated.♥

chocolate-almond truffles

Shown *below* and on *page 145*.

INGREDIENTS

- 1 11½-ounce package milk-chocolate pieces
- ½ cup whipping cream
- ¼ teaspoon almond extract
- ⅔ cup toasted ground almonds
- 4 2-ounce squares vanilla-flavored candy coating
- ½ cup semisweet chocolate pieces, melted

INSTRUCTIONS

1. In a heavy saucepan, combine milk-chocolate pieces and whipping cream. Cook over low heat for 4 to 5 minutes or until chocolate melts, stirring frequently. Remove from heat. Cool slightly. Stir in almond extract. Beat with an electric mixer on low speed until smooth. Cover and refrigerate 1 hour or until firm.

2. Shape chocolate mixture into ¾-inch balls; roll in the ground almonds. Place on baking sheet lined with waxed paper. Freeze for 30 minutes.

3. Meanwhile, in a heavy medium saucepan, melt candy coating over low heat, stirring constantly. Quickly dip truffles into melted candy coating, allowing excess coating to drip off. Place truffles on waxed paper and let stand about 30 minutes or until coating is set.

4. Decoratively drizzle the melted semisweet chocolate over tops of truffles. Store in a tightly covered container in the refrigerator. Makes about 2½ dozen truffles.

Note: For gift giving, include instructions to keep refrigerated.♥

snow folks

Finished sizes vary.
Shown *above* and on *page 147.*

MATERIALS

- Tracing paper
- One pair of cream socks
- 1 red sock
- Scraps of black, orange, and red felt or wool
- 2 4¼"-diameter circles of heavyweight cardboard
- Plastic doll-stuffing pellets
- Polyester fiberfill
- Heavy string
- Plaid wool or flannel: 3x22" strip for scarf, 5x12" rectangle for cape, ¾x8" strip for cap tie
- 24" length of black cord
- Black thread
- 3 black buttons in graduated sizes for coal
- Hot-glue gun and hotmelt adhesive
- Red chenille yarn
- Large-eye needle
- 3 assorted buttons for cap

INSTRUCTIONS

1. Trace the nose and heart patterns, *below right,* onto tracing paper; cut out. From the black wool or felt, cut two ⅝"- and two ½"-diameter circles for eyes. From the red wool or felt, cut one heart. From the orange wool or felt, cut two noses.

2. Remove the cuff from each sock, cutting 1" above the bottom of the ribbing. Set aside one cream and one red cuff for caps. Insert a cardboard circle into the toe area of each cream sock, stretching and smoothing the sock around the edge of the circle. For weight, pour enough plastic doll-stuffing pellets into each cream sock to measure about 1½" deep. Stuff the remainder of each cream sock with polyester fiberfill to within ¾" of the top. Stuff each sock differently, creating a larger snowman and a smaller snowlady. Gather the top of the sock and wrap heavy string around it to secure; knot.

3. To form the neck, squeeze the batting together with your hands. Wrap heavy string around the neck; knot. Tie the 3×22" strip of plaid fabric around the snowman's neck. For the snowlady's cape, fold down 1½" on a 12" edge of the plaid fabric rectangle. Place the black cord inside the fold and wrap the cape around her neck. Tie a bow with the cord.

4. Use black thread to straight-stitch the eyes on the face. For the mouth, fray a 2" to 3" length of fabric thread from the wool or flannel fabric. Referring to the photograph, lay the thread in position on the face and sew in place. Fold the nose in half and sew the long edges together. Trim the seams close to the stitching. Turn right side out and stuff with fiberfill. Sew or glue the nose on the face.

5. Use black thread to randomly straight-stitch the red heart to the snowman's body, referring to the photograph for placement. Glue three buttons to center front of snowlady's body.

6. For the snowman's cap, thread a large-eye needle with chenille yarn and embroider along the finished edge of a cream cuff. Fold up the finished edge 1½" and glue the folded edge to the head. Tie the ¾×8" strip of wool around the top of the cap. Repeat for the red cuff for the snowlady's cap, tying a bow with red chenille yarn. Glue three buttons to the center of the bow. ♥

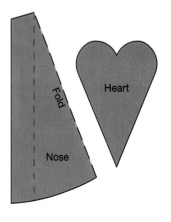

gifts from the garden

gifts of gratitude

gifts for the memories

gifts for the holidays

What the heart gives away is never gone ...

It is kept in the hearts of others.

Robin St. John